I Thought We Agreed To Pee In The Ocean

And Other Amusings From A Girl Wearing Sweatpants

By Alena Dillon

Martlet & Mare Books
Boston, MA

Acknowledgments:

The Big Jewel: Le Tour Defraud
Points in Case: I Thought We Agreed To Pee In the Ocean
Weston Magazine Group: "The Deal Is Off," "On Losing Weight For My Wedding"
The Yellow Ham: "Benedict, By Vatican"
Funny Women of The Rumpus: "The Largest Magazine in the World is No Place for the Likes of Me"
The Huffington Post: "Eat Before the Clock Strikes Fast," "On Defending Myself Against Fame," "The In-Flight Entertainer," and "The Heartache of a Television Serial Dater"
The Dennis Quinn Radio Show: "Dance, Girl"

ISBN: 978-0615844145

Produced in the United States of America

Martlet & Mare Books
Boston, MA

www.martletandmare.com

Contents

Section II: What I Think, And Other Insignificant Contributions to Society

Section III: True Imaginings

i thought we agreed to pee in the ocean

Section I

Then There Was That

Dance, Girl

I was heading up 8th Avenue in New York City, sidestepping empty McDonalds bags, dog excrement, and the occasional homeless person, when a man walking toward me stopped, looked me up and down, and said:

Dance, girl.

I don't strut, saunter, or sway on the streets. I was wearing scuffed up sneakers and a roomy peacoat, and had walked five or six miles, so I was moving more like a truck driver than a showgirl.

Although I don't usually appreciate hearing such requests from strangers, this one made me laugh. Mostly because he said it with so much confidence and with such a supportive sparkle of a smile that I had to believe he'd gotten positive results in the past. The last time he issued the same encouragement, some woman must have stopped in the middle of the crosswalk and whole-heartedly gotten down.

I imagined this man as some manner of groove puppeteer, wandering the streets of Manhattan, scouting out females who could use a little boogie. In my mind's eye, I saw him approaching a worn out middle-aged woman, dragging her heels after a long day at work. The Groove Master, who suddenly had an Afro and aviators, lowered his sunglasses and murmured in a Barry White voice, "Dance, girl." A car drove by blasting Creedence Clear Water Revival, and the middle-aged woman looked down at herself in confusion as her body involuntarily did the grapevine. The confusion didn't last long though, because she soon embraced the jive.

In the Upper East Side, he got a WASP to waltz. Downtown, he got a financier to foxtrot. In Harlem, he got a senorita to salsa. In Chelsea he got a broker to bump and grind. The Groove Master General created movement all across the Big Apple, turning frowns upside down, and plodding into pirouettes.

I wondered if the Groove Master General had a cabinet of officials—a committee of doo-wop do-gooders who wanted the rhythm to get you. Maybe out on these city streets there was a Vice Prance-ident or a Secretary of Step. Did they submit reports to their Groove Master General? Did they have meetings at which they analyzed foot-it footage? When their powers united, did they start flash mobs?

Since we all could use to dance a little more, and in support of the mission of my new friend Sergeant Soul Train and the powers that beat, I rocked a little two-step on my way to Penn Station. My shoulders bounced and my head bobbed.

Then it hit me.

The man didn't say, "Dance, girl." He said, "Damn, girl." And my electric slide powered down to a slouch.

Copy Catcalling

I was sweating to an aerobics video in my apartment. Not just any aerobics video, but *Hip Hop Abs.*

Ten minutes into the workout, while I was popping and locking with all of my might, I heard a whistle coming from outside. I was just wearing a sports bra, so I was practically asking for a whistle. I took it as a compliment and kept on dancing: a little Party Bounce here, a little Night Fever there. Then a few seconds later—another whistle. I rolled my eyes and continued grooving or, as Shaun T would say, "freaking it out." But by the third whistle, I'd had enough. This was a residential neighborhood. Kids lived on this street. What loser was standing outside my window whistling at me? Couldn't a girl sweat in peace? So I asked my husband, Phil, to lower the blinds. As soon as he did, another whistle cut through the air, and now I was furious. The blinds were down, so the guy couldn't even see me. He was just antagonizing.

That's when Phil looked at me and said, "I think it's coming from your DVD."

"It is not!" I said. "It's probably the crazy man that lives on the corner, the guy who walks around his yard wearing only his boxers. He definitely whistled."

"You think we could have heard a whistle from all the way down the block?"

"Obviously we can, since we just did."

"What we heard was a soundtrack."

"That pervert should be locked up."

"Well, why don't you rewind the DVD and see if the whistle sounds at the same exact spot?"

While I rewound the DVD, I already knew Phil was right. Nobody was whistling at me. All that time, I'd been condemning a recording in my living room that would have whistled at me whether I was jumping around in a sports bra or picking rib meat from my teeth.

Sure enough, the whistle was part of the DVD soundtrack.

Now I was thinking: Why *weren't* the neighbors whistling at me? The windows were open and I was hip-hopping around wearing practically nothing. Am I that unappealing that NOBODY, not even The Neighborhood Nudist, thought to whistle? Not even once? I remembered a day before I got married when I sat at a Starbucks window in New York City and a homeless man stood on the other side of the glass, fixed me in his drug-crazed stare, and pleasured himself. I wasn't demanding that criminal level of flattery. Dancing in my apartment in the suburbs, I would have accepted any variety of catcalls. A howl would have been nice. A "hot ass" might have fit the bill. But no. Nothing. A girl standing at an open window in a sports bra couldn't even get a wink.

That neighborhood had no common courtesy. We had to move.

I'm Just Here For The Massage

The chiropractor, a man so petite he'd be turned away from a roller coaster, slid a diagram of the human body across his desk.

"Circle the areas that are bothering you and rate the pain on a scale from 1 to 10," he said.

I picked up a pen, bit my lip, and eyed the diagram. I'd purchased their Groupon for a one hour massage and pain consultation. The trouble was, I wasn't experiencing any pain. I was there for the massage, and the massage alone. I hadn't even acknowledged the pain consultation component until I found myself sitting in a doctor's office, a diagram of the human body under my nose. But I couldn't tell the man with three framed medical degrees that I had no use for his chiropractic expertise, that I just wanted to relax, pure and simple. That I was wasting his time just to get someone to rub me down at the low price of $30. So I put the pen to paper and drew three random circles on the diagram. I faked the pain.

He read over my report and nodded. "What do you do for a living?"

"I'm a writer," I said, pleased because it was the first time I used that as my answer. I don't typically use it since I've only earned $800 writing over eight years of actively working at it, and an average of $100 a year just doesn't add up to career.

"Interesting," he answered, as if it wasn't.

You'd think such a career answer would prompt

the questions, "Oh really? What do you write? Anything I might've read?" And I was disappointed because this doctor didn't need to ask. Somehow, he knew. I hadn't written anything he might've read.

"Well, let me give you a tour of the complex," he said.

We saw the physical therapy room, the gym, the massage therapy room, the physiological therapy room, and the treatment room. This medical facility was about a lot more than aromatherapy candles and Enya. I was in over my head.

We ended the tour in the screening room. "Before I pass you on to our massage therapist, this machine will scan your back and measure the muscle tension. We'll see exactly what the problem areas you marked on the paper look like."

I stared back at him and blinked. "I'm sorry, what the what now?"

"Yes, this is cutting edge technology. The machine is like a muscle x-ray so the massage therapist will know exactly what he's working with."

Which, in this case, was a fibber.

When I drew those circles on the human diagram, pretending I had back issues to get a cheap massage, I'd thought, *What's the harm? How will they know the pain is illegitimate?* Well, here was my answer. This machine was about to scan my muscle tension. My FAKE muscle tension. They were going to hook me up to a chiropractic lie detector. I swallowed so hard I made the cartoon gulp sound.

The doctor handed me a smock and directed me to put it on, open in the back.

When he left the room, I tore off my clothing. I'm not sure what my rush was, but whenever I have to undress at a doctor's office, I move like the doctor is going to turn around and kick the door down. Then I'm left sitting on the examination table wearing the tissue paper gown, panting from the disrobing sprint, my legs swinging. This case was no different. My clothes were strewn across the room, the gown fastened, and I was out of breath. Then I waited for the doctor's return for so long I could've received HP customer support.

It gave me ample time to consider lifting the sofa, just to pull something in my back before it was too late.

The doctor entered after a gentle knock, along with a nurse and a man he introduced as my massage therapist. *Great*, I thought. *My deceit will have an audience.*

Together the four of us stood in front of a large flat screen television. One half of the monitor featured a spine with a corresponding bar graph, indicating the normal level of tension at each vertebra. A blank spine occupied the other half. That was to be my spine. My "aggravated" spine. The nurse dipped two plastic sensors in liquid and pressed them against my top vertebra, while the doctor stood on his tiptoes and held my hair up. Quite the hullabaloo for a discount massage.

"You have right neck pain, so the bar on the right will extend well beyond the normal," the doctor said. He smiled smugly, proud of his new toy.

I decided this was a good time to just run out of the building, but I couldn't spot my shirt.

So I stayed, frozen in place. The medical professionals and the phony watched the bar grow, grow, grow and.... stop—not one millimeter beyond the norm.

There it was, my lie measured.

"Hmm," the doctor said, dropping back down onto his heels.

"Hmm," the massage therapist said.

"Hmm," the nurse said.

"Well that's strange," I said. Although it made the perfect amount of sense.

I worried each of the next 32 vertebral readings would yield the same results—that I had the tension-free back of a newborn baby—and they would see my pain for the con it was. Luckily, it turned out I had muscle tension without realizing it. Unluckily, it wasn't in any of the areas I had circled.

"Maybe muscle tension is having a ripple effect and causing pain in other areas?" I suggested, desperately.

"Maybe," the doctor said, in a tone that implied it wasn't possible.

After the scan was complete, I followed the massage therapist out, staring at the floor like a dog who'd made on the rug.

"Have you ever had a massage before?" he asked.

"Yes," I said, relieved to finally answer honestly.

"Well, this is just like that," he said. "Except I'll actually make you feel better instead of just rubbing random patterns on your back."

And I sighed, because I was no longer the biggest ass in the room.

The Deal Is Off

I'm a Groupon addict.

I've purchased museum tickets, restaurant credit, haircuts, and laser-freaking-eye surgery. I have Groupons stacking up in my account that I'm not sure how I'll ever get around to using, like hotel stays that can only be redeemed midweek, when I, and the rest of the free world, am working.

But I'm now on the road to recovery.

My most recent deal featured a spa offering 50% off scrub or wrap treatments. I had no idea what a scrub or wrap treatment entailed, but they used words like exfoliate, soothing, pamper, and beautify. Most importantly, they used the words "half-off," so I was sold. There were three options, all for the price of $45: the pumpkin scrub, the brown-sugar scrub, or the cellulite-reduction body wrap. The first two were valued at $80 and, while they sounded delicious, the third was valued at $90. Must I say which I chose? This girl loves a deal.

Here's the description for their cellulite wrap: *Cellulite reduction body wraps can significantly improve the shape and tone of your legs, stomach, and buttocks, eliminating cellulite in a single visit.*

You wouldn't have to put a mirror to my thighs to get me to admit that, at twenty-six, my skin is already beginning to ripple. Attribute it to a lack of cardio diligence or the fact that I can tear through half of a large pizza pie without breaking a sweat, but I have dimples in my cheeks, and I'm not referring to my face. So I was intrigued by the idea of a relaxing, rejuvenating treatment while toning up my body without ever having to do a lunge or squat. One click. Bought. The deal is on!

The treatment room was luxurious: candles, classical music, cushioned massage table, the works. And the masseur's Long Island accent wasn't even that whiney. Things were going my way—until the treatment began.

Following the woman's instructions, I undressed and pulled back the sheet on the table, only to find that a material similar to a painter's plastic throw tarp covered the mattress. As I climbed in, it crinkled. I pulled the top sheet over me, feeling like empty paint cans covered up after a long day—if paint cans could have eaten enough Reese's Peanut Butter Cups to give themselves a cellulose problem.

When the masseur reentered, she lifted the bottom of the sheet, and told me she was going to begin with an "aggressive exfoliating peel." Her choice for the first word raised a red flag, but her voice was soothing— a mix between a whisper and a melody. I wonder if the world would be a nicer or creepier place if all words in the vein of "aggressive" were delivered in that same calming tone. "Okay, sir. You're being audited. Take a deep breath, hold it, and let it out nice and slow. That's it. Since you definitely cheated on your tax return and it's only a matter of time before we find out, just imagine your bank account emptying like a trickling stream of penalties."

I forced myself to clear my mind of such stupid speculations, closed my eyes, and sank a little deeper into the mattress, ready to unwind.

As soon as she touched me, I didn't want to open my eyes for fear that I'd confirm she was in fact scrubbing my ass with sandpaper.

I gritted my teeth against the discomfort. She applied the aggressive peel to my butt, abdominal, and upper thighs—the cellulite zones. Tears sprang to my eyes when she touched my inner thighs. I made the mistake of bike riding the day before (okay, I stopped for soft serve along the route), and I may or may not be a person who chafes. When she was finished grinding my skin with crushed pebbles, she toweled it off.

"Now I'm going to apply the toughening gel. It's designed to penetrate your epidermis, or outer skin layer, and break down the fat cells beneath. It may get a little warm. Don't be alarmed, it's supposed to."

Okay, here comes the good part—the massage part, I thought.

She rubbed the gel into the same areas that she applied the rocks of wrath, with the speed and care that one devotes to wiping down a Windexed window. It felt.... okay. When she was through, she stood up and removed the top sheet. Then she took one side of the plastic and folded it over my body. She lifted the other edge, draped it over, and tucked it in. She finished by slipping the bottom under my toes, the way you would secure one end of a turkey wrap. I was swaddled. Mummified. Entombed in gel and plastic. Snug as a bug in a rug. I looked down at myself, and couldn't help but notice the resemblance to one of Dexter's victims.

"All right. This needs thirty minutes to set. I'll come back in fifteen to check in on you," she said and left the room.

I had to lie there like a burrito for thirty minutes. I lifted my head off the bed and eyed my purse, sitting on a chair in the corner, and wished I had asked her for my book. But, since my newest read wasn't within reaching distance and I was essentially sealed inside of a Saran sleeping bag, I decided to make use of the time and brainstorm the characters of a book I was working on. I needed to develop the Chief of Police, figure out her strengths and weaknesses, likes and dislikes, personal history....

Wait, what is this sensation?

From my knees to my sternum, my skin felt as if

it were throbbing from mild sunburn. Certainly uncomfortable, but tolerable.

Well, I'm not menopausal, so it can't be a hot flash. Oh, that's right. The woman said it might heat up. That explains it. Phew! Okay, back to that police chief...

But the sensation intensified, and it was only a matter of minutes before it felt like someone had opened a jalapeño and smeared the seeds over my lower half.

Okay, go to a place of peace. Mind over matter. If you concentrate on the pain, it'll just freak you out more. This is when I opened my eyes for the first time. *Okay, think about how pretty that mirror is with the intricate tiled frame. Or think about what kind of scent that aromatherapy candle is. Jasmine? Lavender? Or think about HOW MY FREAKING LEGS FEEL LIKE THEY WERE DOUSED WITH GASOLINE AND TORCHED!!*

Was this a treatment room or a torture chamber? Jesus. I tried to get a hold of myself. This was a wrap they did every day to many clients. I'm no pansy. I have a high tolerance for pain. If other women could endure this, so could I. Nay, I would enjoy it. I tried to focus on the healing qualities of warmth, to sink into the heat, like you would in a sauna or a hot tub. That was effective for about three seconds. Whatever yogi claimed that you can rise above physical suffering to a state of nirvana has never gotten a cellulite reduction body wrap.

What if the woman did something wrong? What if I was actually experiencing a chemical burn, and when she walked back in here and unwrapped me, my belly and legs were splotched with red and purple discolorations. It would be partly my fault—mostly the fault of the psychopath with a certificate in massage therapy from the New York College of Health Professionals—but also mine because I'm the one who lay here silently and allowed the acid to melt my skin.

Shouldn't I listen to what my body was telling me before I was cooked alive?

But what was I going to do? Call for help? Tell her

that I didn't know what information she wanted, or whom she worked for, but I was ready to talk?

No, ten minutes had to have gone by. I could hold out another five. She'd come back in any second.

I found it hard to breathe.

I thought I might throw up.

Sweat dripped down my sides.

I thought I might throw up again.

In through the nose, out through the mouth. This is a spa. Relax. This is supposed to happen. She'll be back. Just wait.

Waiting.

Waiting.

Torturous, painful, should-be-criminal waiting.

Maybe when we discover that I've been toasted like a Panini, I can sue this spa. I wonder how much I can get. Enough to pay for the skin grafts, sure, but how much extra?

It definitely had been fifteen minutes. Where was the woman? Maybe I should just unwrap myself. Why remain victimized by this European sadistic skin dissolver when I could put an end to the pain. I don't need that woman.

No, it would be embarrassing if she came in and found me lying naked on the table, plastic wrap spewed all around me.

I used my stomach muscles and sat up enough to see the clock. 4:22. If she didn't come back by 4:25, I would break free from this infernal prison.

Burning, burning, burning.

What circle of Hell was this?

4:25. Okay, if she's not back by 4:27, enough is enough.

Burning, sweating, moaning. More burning.

How did I so willingly climb into Satan's envelope? Signed, sealed, and delivered to damnation.

4:27. That was freaking it.

I freed an arm, crossed it over my body, and unpeeled the edge of the plastic wrap. Then, with the opposite arm, I unpeeled the other edge and pulled until the plastic wrap lay beneath me like an open tortilla. The top of my body exhaled, but my bottom half was still being pressed to the hot iron-like plastic, so I placed my feet down on the mattress and pushed off until my butt unstuck itself.

That was my position when the woman finally walked back in: plastic in disarray and me in a nude yoga bridge. She expected to find me lying peacefully in a neat cocoon, and instead I was flailing about, back arched, face writhing, like a person possessed by demons. I'm surprised she didn't turn and call for an old priest and a young priest.

Of course, when she opened the door, she also provided view to anybody and everybody on the other side, but humiliation was drowned out by my ass's much louder shouts of relief.

"What happened?" she asked as she slipped in and shut the door behind her, her eyes wide.

"It got too hot." That was all I could manage. Anything further and I would curse the day she was born.

"I'm sorry! You seemed to be so tough so I let you go the whole thirty minutes without checking in. Did you just take this off?"

I nodded.

"Well, at least you got the full effects then."

"How long do the effects last?" For the amount of torment endured, I expected eternity.

"Three days. Five if you're lucky."

I glanced down at my skin. It looked like one giant welt. I touched it and my thumb left a white fingerprint behind. Their method for reducing cellulite was to irritate your skin into swelling. I might as well have been stung by a hive full of hornets.

So, sorry Groupon, but I've got to cut you cold turkey. I'm not claiming that I won't get withdrawal tremors or dealpression, but that's better than ending up naked on a table in a strange room covered in sweat.

Oh, what's that? 66% off haircut and highlights? The deal is on!

I'm Beginning To Think Strippers Don't Eat Indian Food

I wasn't surrounded by typical exercisers. These women were strippers. They weren't only interested in an increased heart rate and maybe some light socializing. They were there to train. For their work. They could write this class off on their 1040 forms, that is, if they were strippers of the law-abiding, tax-filing variety.

Maybe I shouldn't have been as surprised as I was to find professional entertainers at a pole dancing class. But I'd been to one before, and it wasn't like this.

My girlfriends treated me to a class in New York City for my bachelorette party. At the start, we were encouraged to adopt stripper names. Some of the girls used the adolescent game formula of combining your first pet and street name, but since Shannon 87th Street didn't have the fun sexy edge I was trying to capture, I took the suggestion of the instructor and, as a future bride, went with Diamond.

For all I know, the instructor wasn't just a dance teacher. She may have moonlighted at a place with a name like Booby Trap. She looked the part, anyway, wearing shorts that shared more in common with underwear than outerwear. She had thighs like an Amazon woman and oozed seductive prowess. When we asked her to show off, she climbed a pole to the top of the warehouse ceiling and hung upside down, while the eight of us stared up at her, necks craned, jaws dropped, awed like a bunch of children spotting Santa Claus's sleigh in the sky.

We were civilians. We wore yoga pants and chose bare feet over high heels. We giggled, made silly faces, and struck poses. We didn't take the class seriously. This is not to say we didn't try. I furrowed my brow, trying to figure out how the instructor defied the laws of physics, and gave the basic moves a go. With some practice, I wasn't half bad.

After class, we compared what we affectionately called our "pole burn" and "stripper bruises." It was innocent fun. Folly. And the best exercise I've ever had.

Which is why I wanted to replicate the experience in Long Island.

I found a studio near my apartment through an online directory called Pole Nation: One Nation United By Pole. If this wasn't enough to give me pause, the fact that the business was located in a dingy strip mall on the highway should have been. But I was blinded by hope.

I walked into Sedusa Studios wearing basketball shorts, a white t-shirt that was yellowing under the armpits, and sneakers—not even new, fashionable kicks. Dirty old ones with a peeling sole. My hair was tied in a high ponytail with stray wisps frizzing into tiny hedges at my temples.

The other members of the class wore V-neck sports bras, shorts booty-er than boxer briefs, and stripper high heels (a combination of a block platform front and a stiletto skinny back, aptly named because— and these girls would know—that's what strippers wear). They all let their hair hang loose so that, when they whipped their necks, their manes played a supporting role in the "I'm too sexy for this pole" effect. They looked provocative, and to say that I looked like a stereotypical butch lesbian would be an insult to stereotypical butch lesbians.

While I, the lone island of Long Island, tried to

look busy by stretching a quad here and a trap there, they formed groups around the room, catching up with one another, chatting about who just finished what shift at Blush or Tender Trap. One woman demonstrated for her gal pal a move she'd just perfected. She climbed the pole in two swift pulls, grabbed the steel between her thighs, released one hand and fell backward, gripping the pole with only one set of fingers and her very powerful crotch. It was called the Eye Opener, and it was just that.

Class began with a warm-up the rest of the group was familiar enough with that they had it memorized. You know those nightmares when you show up for school and there's a test you're totally unprepared for, or you arrive to find out it's opening night and you're the star of a play you've never rehearsed? This felt like that. I started in the middle of the room, but by the end of the warm-up I'd made my way to the back corner.

After, the instructor, a beautiful thirty-something, walked around the room and paired people to a pole. She paused in front of me and said, "Are you wearing your micro shorts under there?"

"No, I don't own anything like that," I said.

"Discountstripper.com," she said, and directed me and the closest stripper to me to a pole.

The instructor turned on a stereo that played the kind of R&B where a handful of artists take turns rapping, and since only one of them can sing, they save him for the chorus, while the rest of them add commentary, like, "Hell yeah," and "Yeah baby" and all make sure to state their names for the record.

The moves began easy enough. First we held the pole and strutted around it. Then we swung a little. My partner, a woman with stringy shoulder-length hair and, I assume, daddy issues, and I took turns at the pole. The moves intensified. The other dancers climbed the poles while I sort of jumped at it, clung for dear life, and then slid to the floor like the fat kid on the rope in gym class. As expected, it was a good workout, and I was sweating.

That's when it hit me. A familiar fragrance. Exotic and pungent. Not just body odor, not just something you might expect in a workout environment. There was also something else....

Curry.

Some people misconceive that Indian food tastes like the interior of a taxicab. But I maintain these people have been mistreated by chefs whose talents are as limited as my own. With the correct blend of coconut milk, nutmeg, and ginger, Indian food has the potential to taste like vacation. In what other cuisine can cashews, coriander, cumin, and chilies put aside their differences to create a flavor firework display, bold enough to force diners to set down their forks and appreciate the wonder exploding across their tongues?

My first attempt at homemade Indian food ended in a crash and burn pile of Chicken Tikka Masala smoking embers. Ingredients number one and two on the recipe are yogurt and lemon. Dairy and acid are famous culinary enemies. Thanks to lemon's aggressive position against caseins (protein), it puts poor milk on the curdle train bound for Sour Street. So, it would be natural to blame lemons. It would also be wrong. My problem was apathy. The recipe called for previously grilled chicken to be added to sauce simmering in a pot. But I'm a lazy cook. I chop all ingredients as if I'm preparing stew chunky enough for Jack's Giant, and when I read extra steps or, god forbid, words like "do before" on a recipe, I assume the author is joking, or perhaps just saving her own ass, like when the labels of electronic devices warn you not to do something you would never do, like, "Don't stick your hand in this DVD player while you are taking a bath."

So, when considering the Chicken Tikka Masala recipe, I thought, why grill the chicken? Let's do away with extra steps and get down to business. The pot will get hot. Just throw the chicken into the pot, let it cook, and then add the sauce. It still makes sense to me, even in retrospect, but obviously the Indian people are far wiser than I when it comes to the inner workings of uncooked fowl.

The sauce flavor was fine but, somehow, the chicken tasted too... chickeny. Like biting into a bouillon cube, without the salt. I can't better describe what I mean except that, with every bite, we were acutely aware we were eating poultry, the flavor of pure, unadulterated white meat.

The pain of the Chicken Tikka Masala faded enough in our memory for me to give Chicken Curry with Peas a try. It was a slow cooker recipe where you just toss in the meat, onions, garlic, ginger, curry, cumin and frozen peas, turn the knob, tinker about your apartment and, when you're hungry four hours later, remember you did the whole Crockpot thing. A no-brainer, right?

But the smell of this dish was reminiscent of my family Cockapoo after he escapes and returns from the neighboring marsh. The meal reeked of stewed wet dog, and tasted like one too.

An unfortunate consequence in each of these cases was that I cook in bulk—again, an issue of laziness. If I'm cooking, I'm going to do it once, and it's going to last. Also, I don't throw food away so, when things go wrong, we suffer. Bite, chew, and swallow. Bite, chew, and swallow. Or, as my husband, Phil, calls it, "powering through." Then we look in the refrigerator, see three remaining Tupperware full of wet dog leftovers, and we swallow again.

Over lunch the day after this blunder, I plugged my nose and pushed my way through a bowl of marshy curry—then I went off to the pole dancing class.

As I watched my pole partner execute the fireman spin, knees tucked around the pole and back upright, I snuck a sniff of myself. Yup. It was curry, all right. The spice wafted from my pores and amalgamated with my workout stink.

These were professional exotic artists. Talented strippers. Legitimate athletes. True, one had a sagging gut, but damn she was strong. At one point, she'd climbed a pole, pinched the steel between her bicep and torso, released all four hands and legs, flipped upside down, and hung—held up by only her armpit. And there I was, smelling like Mumbai.

I took my turn at the fireman spin. But my abdominals were too weak to hold an upright fetal position. As I hopped up and sank right back down, the pole squeaking against my skin, the whiff of too chickeny curry rising off my body, I accepted reality. This was not what I'd hoped it would be. It was not a casual place to go exercise and maybe meet some friends. And I was as much a pole dancer as I was a chef of Indian cuisine.

While my partner had practiced her fireman spin four or five times, I was done after the first attempt. I walked toward her and gestured toward the pole, indicating that it was all hers. But as I approached, she wrinkled her nose. Then she walked across the room, away from me, ripped a paper towel from its roll, returned, and wiped down the pole.

I had grossed out a Long Island stripper, a woman who might have gotten naked for a Gotti. I was a Diamond in the rough.

Romance Is Dead. I Killed It

Phil and I started out as friends, and our transition into a relationship was about as smooth as bathtub gin.

On Valentine's Day, which was three weeks into the turbulent evolution, I insisted on setting the mood with greasy food and a horror movie. I hid my anxiety about the date behind a gluttonous mask, thinking that if I kept my hands busy with food, he wouldn't notice that they were shaking.

Like a fat kid on Halloween night, I literally ate myself sick, which I believe entailed consuming four large slices of broccoli pizza and a pint of Ben and Jerry's Cherry Garcia frozen yogurt—as if having full-fat ice cream would have been what made it disgusting. Well, my stomach rejected that amount of food. No more room in the inn.

While Phil kept me company on the bathroom floor, I decided between retches was the perfect time to seal the deal.

"You can be my boyfriend if you want."

I made him an offer he couldn't refuse, and then he held my hair. It was an enchanting evening.

Months later, we were walking to a Connecticut beach on a beautiful, sunny, blue-skied morning when Phil suddenly dropped down on bended knee. My heart stopped. We'd been dating for less than six months! How could he propose this soon? What was he thinking?

My first instinct was to shake my head and run

away. And I did. But after a few steps in the opposite direction, I got a hold of myself. Phil was definitely out of line, but the poor guy deserved more than silent abandonment. He deserved to be let down gently. I had to tell him that, although the answer was no right then, that didn't mean it was always going to be no. He just had to give it some time. Let the relationship grow, breathe. See where things went. This would also be a good time for me to get a sneak peak at his taste in rings so that, if things did continue to go well, I would know whether I had to nip his future purchases in the bud—god forbid he chose a triangle shaped stone or (gulp) yellow gold. I turned around to confront the situation, only to discover—

He was tying his shoe. And I had not played it cool. Laces in hand, Phil stared at me with an expression of bewilderment.

"Where were you going?"

"Who drops down to tie their shoes like that on a beautiful day by the beach with no warning?"

He blinked. Then he smiled. "Did you think I was....? After four months? What am I? Crazy?" He laughed pretty heartily while I wondered what was so crazy and downright hilarious about proposing to me.

Romance makes me uncomfortable. There isn't room enough in my world for the two of us, so when it attempts to surface its pink heart-shaped head, I seek and destroy. I blame it on the pressure. The stakes of ruining a romantic ambiance are just too high. What if, under a star-speckled night sky, prince charming leans in for a kiss at the very moment that I can't suppress a belch? What if we're dining at an elegant French restaurant and while descending the stairs I trip in my heels, tumble, my dress flies over my head, and I expose that I prefer wearing baggy full cheek cotton underwear? What if we're kissing and it's perfect and then I think of that scene in *Friends* when Rachel is making out with Ross and can't stop giggling and then *I* can't stop giggling? That's why I avoid it all. I stay away from star-speckled night skies, elegant restaurants, high heels, and perfect kissing. Nothing gained, true, but more importantly, nothing lost with only myself to blame.

Romantic expectations are as weighty as the expectations of celebrating New Year's Eve—another pressure I can't stand. Society dictates that you've got to ring in the new year with a party the likes of which, earlier in the year, you were previously never cool enough to attend. There's got to be champagne and noisemakers and a guy that's drunk enough to streak through the freshly fallen snow (bonus points if that drunk guy is you).

The scale for measuring the quality of your time is skewed on December 31st. What would have been deemed a pretty good party any other night of the year translates to lame on New Year's Eve. The bar is set so high that anything short of smashing would be considered a disappointment. And so revelers set themselves up for failure, because the chance that you'll find yourself dancing on a table beside a C-list actor until five in the morning is about equivalent to the likelihood that you'll find yourself at a bar among maybe thirteen other people because there's been a blizzard and nobody wants to travel in those conditions, especially when there could be drunk drivers on the road, and it's karaoke night, but everybody is so disheartened by the tepid bar atmosphere that nobody but the karaoke man will sing. And you know the karaoke man had loftier hopes for his career than singing *Captain Jack* at his own karaoke night in a room of thirteen crestfallen drinkers on New Year's Eve.

Since I can't handle the responsibility, I dodge defeat. I arrange intentionally low-key plans for New Year's Eve, and for romance my strategy seems to be— kill the moment right away. Bash cupid's crowning head like an arcade whac-a-mole, lest the situation blossoms into an idyllic fairytale, and THEN I screw things up.

That's why when Phil made a picnic for us on his living room floor, I countered the amorous atmosphere set with candlelight by inciting the following debate: "If you were a vampire, would you turn me?" It seems there is no ideal answer to this question. If you don't turn your partner, it's as good as admitting you'd rather not spend eternity with that person. If you do turn her, you don't love your partner enough to spare her from a forever of human hunting.

Sometimes I destroy involuntarily; maybe I've conditioned my subconscious to sabotage situations. Take the following example:

We were swimming in the ocean when we saw a speck of red every time a wave crested. After the initial scare of it possibly being a bloodstained poisonous jellyfish aiming to suction itself to our hind parts, we realized it was a long-stemmed rose.

You might think there is nothing more romantic than the sight a single rose floating in the sea, but then you've never seen a handsome medium build gentleman of mixed European heritage hopping over waves to retrieve the rose, and then return to present it to you. The image of Phil holding a long stemmed red rose against the backdrop of blue sky and sea was something I'd like to paint, if only I had more artistic flair than a kindergartner with a visual spatial learning disability. It was beautiful, and I was touched. Then a massive wave approached.

In an effort to salvage this souvenir of affection while also not drowning, I submerged myself and thrust my rose-bearing fist into the air. When I resurfaced, with wet hair shrouding my face like the scary she-demon from *The Ring* and sputtering from the salt water that had surged up my nose, I pawed at my mop to clear a path for my eyes, eager to ensure that the flower was still intact.

Nothing remained of the rose but a thorny stem.

Who knows how long it had been drifting at sea in superlative condition, but after one second in my possession, the flower was decapitated, the thickly petaled bud lost at sea, probably bobbing somewhere like a whimsical miniature buoy.

It was such a shame. When I failed to murder romance myself, Poseidon kept me on track. He probably sweetened up some sultry water deity with his trident and his slick abs and my rose bud, that son of a beach.

My mission to destroy sentimentally forged onward. I had this sneaking suspicion that Phil was going to propose. We'd gone ring shopping and I saw him swipe his credit card and everything. I had one more year of graduate school remaining before I had to pursue a full time job with potentially limited vacation time, so we realized that if we wanted a longer honeymoon, we'd have to get to committing, and what better reason to get married than an extended vacation? (In retrospect this reasoning was flawed. Not because there are better reasons to be wed, but because three years later I still don't have a full time job).

Anyway, while waiting for the proposal, I continually ruined Phil's plans by painting mental pictures of incredible proposals that, unbeknownst to me, he was already putting into motion.

"You should take me to that waterfall in the woods and we'll have a picnic on a rock!"

"You have GOT to be kidding me," he said. Back to square one. This happened twice more but, on the bright side, we confirmed that we shared similar tastes.

When the time came, he got down on both knees and presented me with my ring, nestled in the folds of a silk rose he'd made himself. Then we feasted on a heart-shaped broccoli pizza, and I managed not to regurgitate it, which spells success on my scale.

I may not be a perfect woman, I may be a romance sabotaging she-klutz, but Phil said that I'm the perfect woman to him, and that's as perfect as it can get.

Letters From A Brawd

I don't mean to brag, but I excel in designing vacations in which, upon landing in a different country, of a different time zone, that speaks a different native language, I arrive completely stranded. No matter how far in advance I reserve a hotel, Phil and I inevitably end up standing on a foreign cobblestone street bearing nothing but useless confirmation emails and sleep deprivation.

Take our honeymoon, June 2011. We went to Athens, figuring nothing celebrates a union better than a protest-ridden city on the brink of seceding from the union. You say walks on the beach and candlelight dinners? I say riot shields and tear gas.

At the airport, I handed a taxi driver the address (Timoleontos Vassou 22) of our destination—a 4.5 star luxury boutique hotel called The Angel Suites. It took the man a while to maneuver the city center, given that many streets were packed with screaming Maalox-painted demonstrators. When we initially drove past them, in my foreign affairs ignorance I chirped, "Oh look, a street fair." Hopefully the cabbie thought I just had a very dry sense of humor.

I wasn't familiar with Athens but, after a while, even I knew we were driving in circles. And why was the driver looking in confusion from the hotel information to the buildings and back?

He pulled the cab to the side of the road in front of a Best Western. "I'll be back," the Arnold

Schwarzenopoulos said with a nervous smile and then hopped out of the cab, taking our email confirmation paper with him. Phil and I looked at each other and shrugged. We had been traveling for twelve hours. Slathered in plane grease and exhaustion, he could have said he just needed to run in and smash some plates and we would have thought it a reasonable pit stop.

Five minutes later he returned, popped his trunk, and removed our luggage.

"Excuse me, sir? I don't think this is our hotel. Our hotel is called The Angel Suites," I said.

He again flashed me that nervous smile. "Yes. Talk to the lady. She will tell you." He dropped our two luggage pieces inside The Best Western and he and his cab were halfway back to the airport before he finished the sentence.

Inside, The Lady informed us in broken English that this was indeed the correct address, but that the hotel we reserved in August the previous year was bankrupted in September. The Best Western replaced it in January and The Angel Suites, The Best Western, and our travel agent all assumed one of the previously mentioned parties would catch us up to speed. Yes—we reserved a hotel for our honeymoon, it closed, and nobody thought to tell us about it. It was now June, at 4 am our time, we had been up all night, were in a foreign city, and had nowhere to stay for the next week.

"Well, do you have any room at this inn?" I asked, lip trembling. The Lady did not.

After a soggy breakdown in which I whined, "But this is our honeymoon" at a pitch only the stray dogs roaming The Acropolis could hear; a two hour nap on The Best Western lobby sofa; several angry emails to our travel agent; and a spanakopita (spinach and cheese filled pastry); arrangements were made at a hotel across the city, and we were shuttled through a mob of protestors to arrive at higher-rated facility that hadn't bankrupted and featured a working elevator. We enjoyed free breakfast, two free nights, and the rest of our trip.

A year later, swap a *kalimera* for a *bonjour* and a *spanakopita* for a *crepe* and Phil and I had some Pepe le Pew style déjà vu.

On this trip across the Atlantic, we were scheduled to stay in a woman's Paris apartment. We would soon learn that this woman didn't understand the critical value in being at the apartment when we arrived. We called her from a payphone and were dismayed by the sound of her voicemail. After waiting with our luggage in front of a locked door for fifteen minutes, we went forth to find Internet, thinking maybe she emailed us about being late.

Manhattan is designed using the same philosophy college campuses apply to Emergency Call Boxes—from any given Starbucks, a caffeine seeker can locate her next source of skinny vanilla lattes. I hoped Paris had been inspired by our ugly consumerism, so we dragged our luggage down the street, searching for a Starbucks, American's favorite Wi-Fi hot spot.

Voila! A Starbucks! Oh, but the Internet was broken that day. Where was the nearest Internet cafe? Around the corner! Magnifique! Oh, but it was closed.

Feeling desperate, I walked into a small hotel across the street from the Internet cafe. Behind the desk sat a woman with a bun tied so tight that I worried, if undone, her face might fall off.

"Excuse me, do you have Internet here?"

"Yes. But only for customers."

"I have nowhere to go. I need to get in touch with the person I'm staying with. Can I pay you to use the Internet for ten minutes?"

"No. There is Internet across the street."

"It's closed."

"So?"

So? So? So what the hell am I supposed to do? I have nowhere to go, no way to contact this lady. Help me, si vous freaking plait!

"Okay, well, do you have any room here?"

"No."

Madame Misery needed to pull the baguette from her basket.

We dragged our feet—and our luggage—back to the apartment. Still no answer.

A woman with a cloud of white hair appeared from next door. She said something in French, and we said something in English. She motioned inside of her apartment. We peeked into the doorway and, when our eyes adjusted to its cavernous lack of lighting, we found a dog the size of a small horse and enough clutter to qualify her for a segment on A&E. I didn't know what she fed her pet to sustain such an enormous creature, but she seemed a little too friendly to be both well-meaning and French. We smiled and said *merci* but no *merci*. We'd rather not be murdered and fed to a mutant canine so far from home.

Having floundered during the Internet journey, we embarked on a separate but similar quest for a telephone. This odyssey ended half a block away at a hostel masquerading as Practic Hotel, which I assume was short for practically a hotel.

We walked into the dark lobby and, behind a mahogany desk, sat a thirty-something man who looked like a spy movie villain that was fated to be outwitted.

"Excuse me, do you speak English?"

"Yes."

"Would it be possible to use your phone?"

"Yes, but you must first wait," he said, as if this were obvious and we had just violated basic French protocol. He gestured into a room across the hall, where we found a bored looking bald man sitting in an uncomfortable chair. We rolled our luggage across the hall and... waited.

The doomed villain shuffled some papers around. He looked out the window. He tapped his fingers on the desk. A smudge caught his eye, and he polished it with his sleeve. He glanced at his watch.

"Okay, come in," he said, and the bald man did.

(We would come to find that this was the villain's signature move. No matter how simple our question, he would find some pencils to organize so that we could spend our due time in the waiting room before he addressed us. Talk about a Napoleon complex.)

Either the phone system was far too complicated for our American minds to wrap around or the villain didn't want to have to disinfect the keypad after our dirty American fingers touched it because he waved anxiously for the number, dialed it himself, and then passed me the handset.

While the phone rang, the hopeless villain shot me a glare that said, "This call better be good. I have a stapler to straighten." Alas, I got voicemail.

I left a message that said something like, "Hi, this is Alena Dillon, the person who paid you money in exchange for sleeping in your apartment this week. I'm here, and I'm just wondering where you are." The subtext being, "Are you f****** kidding me??"

When I passed the handset back to the receptionist man, his glare transformed into an expression of smugness, as if he knew all along the phone call was a waste of his precious tinkering time.

"Well, I guess we have nowhere to go," I said. "Do you have any room here?" I asked the man.

He rolled his eyes. "Well, yes. But, please—" He pointed to the room across the hall. "—you must wait."

So we spent the night at the Practically-a-Hotel Hotel. We schlepped our luggage up five flights of a winding staircase and slept in a room that I would have sworn was an underground dungeon if I hadn't still been wheezing from the climb up. We opened the door, shimmied sideways down a short, narrow hall that led to a room exactly the dimensions of its king size bed. The bathroom was so tiny that when I sat on the toilet I scraped my knees against the wall. That place must have been where they imprisoned the Count of Monte Cristo. Oh, *pardonne moi. Le Comte de Monte-Cristo.*

I regress into a tired child when exhausted by

travel. Everything around me looks yucky, but all is better after a nap and a snack. After we passed out in the Practic Hotel and woke up to have a crepe, the apartment owner reached us and the issue was resolved. She claimed we must have kept missing each other, but I knew that was a bunch of *merde* because we don't live in a Scooby Doo haunted hotel where Shaggy and Scoobs open doors and run down the hallway into other rooms while ghosts do the same, and their paths miraculously never intercept. Still, she refunded the cost of the first night and I let the issue lie—we'd already wasted too much vacation time mopping up my disappointment.

The rest of our week was a prixe fixe meal of French culture served with a glass of Bordeaux. Okay, a bottle.

I'm beginning to learn that sometimes, even if you book trips over a year in advance and have all of your travel documents in a folder in the order that you'll need them, it isn't enough. Sometimes, *merde* happens. And you have to relinquish control. Roll with the punches. Make the best of the practically a hotel hotel.

That, or just double book for the first night.

The Stink Of Death

About a year ago, our landlord decided that the regal oak standing guard on the plot between the sidewalk and the street was dropping too many leaves on his lawn, so he hacked it down. That was the reason he claimed, anyway. The truth is that our area of south shore Long Island can only take so much natural beauty, so the tree had to be removed and a tattoo parlor erected, all to please the concrete gods.

Phil and I mourned the loss of the majestic oxygen-maker. If we had known beforehand, perhaps we would have picketed outside to protest or assembled a rally of all our local friends: Phil, me, and my childhood stuffed husky. Alas, we did not, and one day we came home to find nothing but a stump and a pile of sawdust.

Sure, we were disappointed, but there was an upside: the army of pigeons that cooped in that oak lost their home and had to relocate (incidentally, to the neighbor's roof), meaning our car windshields would be met with a lot less bird droppings.

But we underestimated the consequences.

In the days immediately following the tree execution, we noticed the pungent smell of dog poop when climbing into our car. Phil and my conversations while in that vicinity sounded like the lyrics to a Lynyrd Skynyrd song. "Oh, that smell! Can you smell that smell?" At first I didn't think too much of it; my landlord had a German Shepherd. So for a few days we watched where we stepped and inspected our shoes before entering our apartment. But then I remembered that the German Shepherd had been dead for three months. The smell was not dog poop. It was decaying tree stump.

We aren't talking about a mild odor here. It was a concentrated stench, a complex mélange of rot, earth, and the stuff that rotting earth rejects. Like dried fecal matter and spiced compost with not very subtle echoes of death. You would think that the insides of a tree, which have essentially been aged in oak barrels, would smell more like wood and less like zombie breath.

And whenever we headed in the direction of the stump, the wind picked up, whistled the sound of God's laughter, and delivered the aroma directly into our nostrils.

For ten months (through the winter! Cold air doesn't often carry stench, but it made an exception for the stump) we held our breath each time that we entered and exited our cars, until one day when I pulled up to the curb and found the stump replaced by a mound of mulch. I literally clapped and squealed, so happy was I that the reign of the stinky stump was over. Then I stepped out of the car, and the funken odor grabbed me by the cheeks and pressed its mouth over my nose.

Grinding the stump into bits only pissed it off. That's how I explained it anyway. Phil said that now more surface area was exposed to emanate the fragrance. And emanate it did. Now the rot was rotting and the death was dying. We went from holding our breath from car door to front door to requiring a HAZMAT suit.

Phil is hopeful, though. Apparently now that the stump is powder, it will decompose quicker. The question is whether or not we will still be here to "reek" the benefits.

Like A Spider Waiting For the Kill

I spotted the Mister Softee truck on the corner of Fifth Avenue and 13th Street and experienced the familiar swell in my chest. When sixty hours a week of your life are miserable, you have to cling to the bright blips to survive. They are your life raft in a sea white-capped with anxiety.

I didn't have enough money to afford my own apartment. Hell, I didn't have enough money to afford my own bed. But I made room in my budget for ice cream cones. They didn't just nourish my stomach; they nourished my soul.

Each day, I worked my way through the sugary sprinkles, as if giving the exterior a fresh face. Then I lapped at the creamy soft serve, savoring it, while admiring the brownstones on West 12th Street. *Would the city be kinder if I could afford to live in one of these residences? If that pot of geraniums on the front steps was mine to water? Well, at least I have my ice cream. My steadfast comfort.*

By the time I snapped off the first chunk of wafery cone, I was rounding 6th Avenue, leaving the quiet neighborhood behind and reentering the commercial world. As I turned back on 14th Street, the cup of the cone was gone and only the vanilla filled stem remained. I passed a Starbucks, an Urban Outfitters, and a New York Sports Club.

Standing back in front of my building, I took the last bite, where the cone was softest and the treat melted against my tongue in an ode to sweet cream. And that was it. My break was over, my cone gone, and I had to go back to work, my only hope being tomorrow's lunchtime dessert. Ice cream cones were the fresh cool water on my parched lips.

Following many interviews at many companies, some six-hours, some shorter than a cigarette break, and some held in sketchy apartment buildings by people only pretending to offer legitimate employment, I got a job. It sounded promising: Administrative Assistant for a public relations firm. A place I thought I could grow. I was wrong; it would make me cower.

On my first day of work, I aimed to appear professional—pretending that I wasn't just out of college, that I knew how to walk in heels, that New York City and the stockings I kept yanking up my thighs fit me comfortably.

Then the flowers arrived.

When the deliveryman knocked and entered the office carrying a large bouquet, it didn't register that the flowers could be for me, which is why I naively said, "Oh, flowers! Who are they for?"

The man reached around the bundle of roses and pulled a card from the stems.

"Dear Alena. Good luck on your first day," he read. "We know you'll find success in all that you do. We love you. Mom and Dad."

I pictured my dad, my teddy bear patriarch, crying into his keyboard when he placed the order—the order that melted my professional façade, revealing me for what I was: a fraud in a pant suit. A little girl who made her parents proud.

The bouquet demanded the larger part of my desk. I maneuvered around them awkwardly until they wilted forty-eight hours later—and I swear their swift death was because joy couldn't survive in that office—at which point the boss, let's call her Cruella, grumbled, "Ditch the flowers."

I'd been working at her company for a week when she walked past my desk, saying without stopping, "Make me a reservation for four at Le Cirque tonight at 7:30."

"Okay!" I chirped. Only when she was safely inside her office, door closed, did I exhale.

I googled Le Cirque's phone number and dialed. When a woman answered, I requested the reservation.

"I'm sorry. It's restaurant week. Le Cirque is booked. We have availability at ten o'clock, but that's it. We don't have a prime dinner hour slot open until next month."

I whispered a "Thanks anyway," so Cruella wouldn't hear my failure, and gently placed the phone in the cradle.

Crap, crap, crap! I can't go into Cruella's office and tell her I was unsuccessful. Her eyes will laser beam me to death. Okay, okay. It's not your fault. I mean, what could you do? Maybe she didn't realize it's restaurant week. Maybe she'll understand.

I took a few deep, calming breaths and eyed her office door. *You can do this. And she can't physically hurt you, so what's there to be afraid of?*

I stood, cracked my knuckles, walked toward her door, and tapped the glass.

"What?" Cruella asked.

I opened the door a slice and peeked through. "Le Cirque is booked. It's restaurant week."

"I know it's restaurant week. That's why I wanted to eat there. I'm a New Yorker, you think I don't know it's restaurant week?"

"The woman said there's a ten o'clock tonight or a seven o'clock next month."

"Oh, for God's sake."

Maybe she actually could physically hurt me. My butt cheeks clenched.

"Fine. Get me a reservation at Aldea."

I repeated Aldea under my breath so I wouldn't forget it. I sat at my desk and googled Aldea's number. I dialed, praying, literally praying, there'd be availability. If there wasn't, I might consider jumping out the window. I could probably survive the fall if I grabbed some tree branches on the way down. When the woman picked up, I requested the reservation.

"You know it's restaurant week, don't you?" the woman asked. "You can't get a 7:30 day-of. You can't even get a ten o'clock day-of."

"Please?" I squeaked.

"Sorry, we're booked. I can try to fit you in next week."

I hung up, trying with all my might to keep the giant FUCK screaming inside my head, inside my head.

I eyed her door again, the door to hell. I ran through my options, which didn't take long because I didn't have many. 1) The window idea. 2) I could tell Cruella she didn't have a reservation. 3) I could quit. Just leave the office and never come back. At least then I wouldn't have to see the look on her face when I told her Aldea is booked.

No, she hired you for a reason. You write a good press release. So you don't have pull at the biggest restaurants in town. That wasn't on your resume. What does she expect?

I looked down at my hands. They were trembling. And I was sweating. All over a reservation.

I tapped on the glass again.

"What?"

I opened the door a crack.

"I don't want to hear Aldea is booked," Cruella said.

Now I wasn't sure what to do. Go back to my desk? Say it anyway? "Um, okay."

"You couldn't get a reservation?"

"No."

"Fine. If you're too incompetent to get a reservation at any restaurant in New York City, I'll do it myself."

"Okay, sorry," I said. I closed the door and went

back to my desk to let the rest of my panic attack run its course. I was wheezing. I knew I should have brought my inhaler.

After a moment, Cruella's door opened. I snapped into perfect posture and typed randomly on the keyboard to look busy.

"I got a reservation at Le Cirque," Cruella said, looking simultaneously smug and annoyed.

"For 7:30?" I asked.

"Yes."

My butt cheeks clenched. "How?"

"I told them who I am. Why didn't you just tell them who I am?"

How was I supposed to know you are anybody? I'd never heard of her before. You aren't exactly on the cover of National Enquirer hugging your adopted African children. "Gosh, sorry. I'll lead with that next time."

Gosh? Gosh? Why the hell did I pick right now to introduce that word into my adult vocabulary for the first time? Who do I think I am, Theodore Cleaver?

Cruella nodded, annoyed. "Next time, I'll accept perfection."

The commute from my parents' house to work, between Metro North, the subway to Union Square, and walking to the office, took just about two hours. I left the house at seven and didn't get home until eight. That gave me two hours to cry about my sorry life before going to bed for another early morning. But in an economy where hundreds, maybe thousands, of graduates were waiting for me to screw up so they could take my desk, what choice did I have? I was starting a career.

Fortunately, my friend Michelle sympathized. She lived in the East Village, only six blocks from my office, and offered to let me stay at her apartment during the week until I found a place of my own. Perhaps she was only being polite, but I embraced her proposal like a desperate spinster.

So, Monday morning, I boarded Metro North armed with clothes for the week and two large containers of frozen soup. The soup was to be rationed out as lunch throughout the week. I would soon learn that everybody in the office ordered lunch out, and certainly nobody defrosted beef stew brought from their mother's freezer in Connecticut. This would not deter me from continuing the practice. Apparently my bank account was a higher priority than my reputation.

With all of its contents, the size of the overnight bag was clumsy. It demanded its own seat on the train and knocked people in the subway—and not lightly considering inside were two ice broth bricks. Commuters in Manhattan were naturally nasty, especially in the morning, without being slugged by my frozen lunches. If looks could kill, I was murdered repeatedly on that morning commute—and then repeatedly throughout the week by The Accepter of Perfection. Come Friday morning, worn and beaten down, I'd leave Michelle's apartment to head back to Connecticut, lugging dirty clothes and empty soup containers. On the train ride home, I was more than once so dejected that I passed out on the shoulder of a neighboring businessman, and slept soundly enough that he had to nudge me back to consciousness to say, "Sorry, but this is my stop."

Living out of a bag Monday to Friday meant that I wore the same pair of pants two or three days in the week, and Cruella noticed.

"Elaine, I pay you enough that you can afford to buy some new work clothes."

Actually, she didn't. "I know, I'm sorry. I just have a lot of loans to pay off," I said. Actually, I had no loans, only fear.

"By the way, are you living in the city yet?"

"Um, yes," I said. "Just moved in." I didn't want to get into the details about being one socio-economic class category above a hobo.

"Good," Cruella said. "Now you won't have to dash

out of the office at 5:30 on the dot. Try staying until six or seven once in a while. It won't kill you." Actually, I already did and, actually, it might.

Bless Michelle's heart, she let me sleep, beside her in her bed, for four months. This is not to say I didn't look for apartments. I did. But I made $500 a week. Rooms in Manhattan were $2,000 a month, and I wasn't sure I could survive on nothing.

There were a few sublets in my price range:

"$106 a month for a bedroom near St. Mark's Place. Room is quite large with a private bathroom. Certain stipulations apply. Roommate must be an 18 to 25-year-old female in good shape. For such low rent, I will require female to occasionally walk around in her underwear. No sexual contact is necessary. Just wash a few dishes wearing only your bra and panties once in a while. I'm not a creep. I'm just a businessman so consumed with work, I don't get out much. I'd like to bring some excitement into my apartment. Interview necessary."

I passed on this listing. Aside from the obvious reasons, I had additional concerns. What would happen when the renter turned twenty-six? Would she be evicted? Or what if she gained a little weight? Would plumping restrictions be in the lease agreement? Also, what did he mean by, "No sexual contact is necessary"? If the tenant was willing, could there be further rent negotiations, or did he just consider it a roommate relationship perk, like when both inhabitants enjoy watching the same television shows or are both vegetarians? Another disturbing detail was the arbitrary rent number. Why not a nice round one hundred bucks? He must have been weird. Plus, only creeps find the need to say, "I'm not a creep."

"I am a female in my mid 60's looking to rent out a large bathroom in my one-bedroom Harlem home. You can easily put a twin air mattress in there. I only ask that when I need to use the bathroom, you and your air mattress aren't in it. When you are in the apartment, you must confine yourself to the bathroom. I do not feel comfortable having a stranger walking around my living room. You may have guests over as long as they are confined to the bathroom as well. This might seem a bit odd, but please remember the rent is $400 and the bathroom is large. Cats are okay."

Harlem was up and coming, but $400 a month to abide in a tiled health code violation seemed a little steep. So I stayed in Michelle's bed.

Email from Cruella: Alani, I'm going to the Hamptons Friday morning. I want SoandSo's tour schedule forwarded to me five minutes before you receive it.

Email from Me: You got it, Cruella. Have a great weekend!

Email from Cruella: Soandso's schedule is in Word. It should always be in Excel. You should know this, Alaina. Also, never use an exclamation point in an email to me again.

Email from Me (Saved to drafts and then deleted for fear it might accidentally get sent): Sorry!!!!!!!! PS. My name is ALENA!!!!

After a month, I cried at work. One of our clients, an alcohol brand, was releasing coffee-infused vodka. I wasn't assigned to this account, but Cruella asked me to rewrite its press release. This was strange since, up until then, I'd been restricted to three other accounts. But I would never question Cruella. If she wanted to shave my head, I'd hand the woman a razor.

The original author of the press release chose a cutesy barista theme. Cruella loathed it. I knew she loathed it because she said, "I loathe this." She didn't know what she wanted the angle to be, but it wasn't that. She told me to do something with it and give it to Anne for approval. Anne, the vice president, was slightly less intimidating than Cruella.

After I'd rewritten it, I went into Anne's office.

"Here's the press release Cruella asked me to do," I said, handing her the paper.

"What press release?" she asked, taking the paper slowly.

The color rushed to her face; I knew I was in trouble. "The coffee vodka press release," I said, tentatively.

She smacked her lips. "I didn't know she was having you revise the press release we've revised for her five thousand times," Anne said, slicing each word into a staccato. Then, cleaving me with her stare, she crumpled my press release into a tight ball and threw it on the floor. It bounced off my boots.

I looked down at my shriveled work. Was I supposed to bend over and pick it up? No, that would be pathetic. "Um, okay," I said and walked out of her office, leaving the release on the floor.

I grabbed my coat and left for my thirty-minute lunch break. As soon as the crisp Manhattan air swept me into its arms, I released my sob. Cruella had turned us against each other. She wasn't our only enemy; we were each other's enemy as we fought for success and corporate approval. I understood Anne's frustration. She, the vice president, needed her press release rewritten by the new admin?

I took long strides up Fifth Avenue toward the Empire State Building. Was this what I wanted for myself, for my career? To climb this fierce ladder? To compete, to step on the hands of my coworkers, albeit unintentionally? What must the grand view be like from the top? I imagined miles and miles of uppity restaurants that would squeeze me in during restaurant week, and piles and piles of people I crushed along the climb. Eh, who was I kidding? I'd end up being one of the casualties that some much more qualified, hardworking, colleague left behind on rung two. Still, I got vertigo just thinking about it.

I turned off Fifth toward Union Square. There was

a farmer's market there every Thursday. I roamed through stands of jams, breads, soups, and fresh vegetables—vegetables that had to have been grown outside the city and brought in for sale.

Conversation with coworker while riding the subway on the way to the screening theater to drop off new film:

Me: So, Cruella is something, huh?

Coworker: Yeah, isn't she a rock star?

Me: (pause) You know she can't hear us, right?

All the girls in the office drank coffee. They had cups delivered in the morning and afternoon, because anything can be delivered in Manhattan, even $1.50 cups of coffee. I was doing the same until I realized that three dollars a day, five days a week, is fifteen dollars. That's sixty dollars a month, and for sixty dollars a month, I could buy a week in a Manhattan bathroom. After writing and rewriting an email to Cruella, I asked permission to bring in a coffeemaker for office use.

Cruella replied, "I suppose, as long as you keep it clean. And in the future, just come into my office for these kinds of questions. I don't bite."

Ha.

The next week, I brought in a French press my mom wasn't using and Godiva coffee grounds, again, that my mom wasn't using. Does it get any fancier than an Italian brewing device named after the Parisians and a century old gourmet Belgian chocolate company? I didn't think so but hell, what did I know?

Cruella walked by. She lifted the Godiva bag between her fingers and held it away from her body with an outstretched arm. She dropped it in the trashcan.

"What was that crap? Alana, here's twenty bucks. Don't poison the girls. Buy Illy. We only drink Illy."

When she closed her office door behind her, I grabbed the coffee grounds from the garbage and stuffed them into my purse.

I was working on website copy for a winery when a nice old lady walked into the office. I looked up and smiled, certain she had the wrong door.

"Can I help you?"

She looked at me warmly. "You must be Alena. So nice to finally meet you." She extended her hand and I shook it. Her skin was as soft as rabbit fur. She smelled like oatmeal cookies. "I'm Susan, Cruella's partner."

I almost recoiled.

No, it couldn't be. This good woman, this lovely creature who probably made a fine banana bread and loved her cat, voluntarily shared a home with Cruella? This sweet granny, this Mrs. Claus, was Cruella's lifemate? Didn't she know Cruella was part Satan? Didn't she see that Cruella was the lovechild of Ursula and Captain Hook?

"So nice to meet you, Susan. Cruella's in her office." *Don't look directly into her eyes or you'll turn to stone. But hey, you knew that.*

I itched to leave my chair on Friday evenings. To be rid of the PR prison. To run wild and free. To breathe deeply without worry of consequence. To sing and twirl and laugh like Julie Andrews. Over the weekend, I had nightmares about Cruella, about mistakes I made that she discovered. She had me in her office and there was no escape. Her belly laugh was rumbling and evil as she approached me in the corner. I watched her shadow grow on the wall.

I woke with a gasp, clammy from head to toe. But oh, it was only a dream. Then I'd remember it was Sunday night. Tomorrow was Monday, and the dread rolled back fiercely.

We represented one famous person who owned a handful of hotels, which Cruella and I handled exclusively. When Cruella was on business trips, I was the only individual in the office who knew anything about the hotels.

The phone rang. It was Maria, the manager at the new, exotic Colombian hotel.

"I need to speak to Cruella."

"She's in flight at the moment."

"Then you need to help me."

"Uh, okay."

"There's a journalist here. He says he's supposed to come in, photograph the hotel and do a piece on it. I wasn't told anything about him. Should I let him in or turn him away?"

"I wasn't told anything about a journalist either. Maybe we should wait for Cruella's flight to land."

"No. He's at the door. I need to give him an answer now. If he leaves, he may not come back."

"I've only worked here for two months. I can't make that kind of decision. You decide."

"You are the PR company. You have to make this decision."

I tapped a pencil on the desk, knowing this situation could go horribly wrong. If I told Maria to let him in, maybe he would print the write-up in a publication Cruella deemed not worthy of doing a piece on the hotel. But if Cruella arranged this, and I told Maria to turn him away, and Cruella loses press she actually wanted, well, I'd rather risk the window jump. I decided getting unwanted press was the lesser evil than losing desired press.

"I don't know, Maria. Let him in, I guess."

I hung up the phone, feeling relieved, feeling satisfied with myself for fielding a high-pressure situation with a normal amount of shaking and sweats. Maybe I wasn't so bad at this job after all. Maybe I *was* a New York career woman!

On Monday morning, Cruella was back in the office and I received an email in my inbox reading, "My office. Now."

I coaxed my Gumby legs to move one in front of the other until I reached her door. Tap tap.

"What?"

I opened the door. "You wanted to see me?"

"Sit." She pointed to a seat in front of her desk. I would have preferred the electric chair. I sat and pressed a fingernail into my palm for distraction. "You gave Maria permission to let an unauthorized journalist into the Colombian hotel?"

Oh, fuck. "Well, first I said I didn't know. That I couldn't make that decision. But she said neither could she. Somebody needed to make the call, and I didn't think you'd want a journalist turned away. Press is so precious," I said.

"Who are you to give permission to anybody for anything? You're just an administrative assistant. You've been here for two months. You. Are. Nothing."

I stared into my lap. "I didn't know what to do."

"I've fired people for much less. Do you realize that?"

I nodded.

"Do you want to be fired? Is that why you made that stupid, presumptuous decision?"

Did I want to be fired? Of course! No recent college graduate with dreams of happiness wants to spend sixty hours per week with her butt cheeks clenched. So did I want to be put on unemployment, and earn part of my paycheck while maintaining a safe sixty-mile distance from the devil incarnate? Hell. Yes.

But did I want to be a failure on my first big try? Did I want to trudge home on Metro North only to admit to my parents that four years of college tuition and twenty dollars spent on 1-800-Flowers for my congratulatory bouquet was all for naught?

"No."

"You're lucky nobody else in this office can write worth a damn. Otherwise, I would fire you. I wouldn't lose sleep over it." She nodded toward her door. "You can leave now."

I nodded and left her office. I continued past my desk, out the door, down the elevator, and out onto the city streets. I needed release. I needed my ice cream cone.

I quickened my step, crossed the street, and approached the ordering window.

But it was closed.

I lifted onto tiptoes to spot the man within. Empty.

Then the ice cream truck started moving. Not providing me with my vanilla cone with rainbow sprinkles, but moving. Taking my daily taste of happiness with it. I would have to return to another five hours of clenched butt cheeks and stress headaches without the comfort of creamy residue on my tongue.

This could not be. I would not make it.

I pounded on the tin exterior with both fists, and it reverberated like a drum. My lips parted, and I did not recognize the sound that rose from my belly and poured from my mouth, like an injured wookiee's cry before surrendering to death.

I was twenty-two, and banging on an ice cream truck. This was rock bottom.

The truck stopped. And reversed a little. Then the engine died. I sucked in the kind of rattled breath that is mixed with a sob.

The man appeared inside the truck and opened the window.

"Wow, somebody really needed an ice cream cone," he said.

"Vanilla with rainbow sprinkles," I said. "Make it a double."

When I turned around, holding a cone in each hand, I found two attractive and put-together twenty-somethings on their lunch breaks, finishing up the ice cream cones they secured before the truck almost pulled away, laughing at me. Not even trying to hide it for the sake of courtesy. Openly in hysterics.

I forced a smile in return, while the mental image of what I'd done, of what I'd been reduced to, replayed in my head. I just pounded on an ice cream truck like a medieval criminal being chased by a feral crowd of torchbearers would beat on the doors of a cathedral, desperate for the law of sanctuary. I pounded on that ice cream truck as if a vanilla cone with rainbow sprinkles was the only thing that could save my life.

This was me. This was what I'd become.

Before I got the job, my family had booked a vacation to Florida. Cruella allowed me to take it, unpaid, which was fine because, by that time, three months into the job, I would have paid *her* to let me go.

Lying on the sand, I sighed like I'd been holding my breath for three months, as if every muscle in my body had been clenched, and now I was finally releasing. Not until I had the distance, until I had the juxtaposition, did I realize how unhappy I really was. It occurred to me as I sipped a piña colada that I had a choice. I wasn't bound to this job. It wasn't a sentence. I could leave. I whispered this realization out loud, like it was the answer to the meaning of life. "I should quit," I said. I was on to something. Freedom. "I should go to graduate school."

Back in New York, I sported a tan and a bounce in my step. Life seemed worth living again. I spent Monday applying to three grad schools, minimizing the Internet window whenever a coworker walked by. My application, including the personal essay, was completed and submitted by Tuesday. I was accepted a month later.

May 29th. The date was circled in red and adorned with bold exclamation points in the calendar of my brain. My last day. I could almost taste freedom on my tongue. I could almost remember what it was to feel hope. May 29th. Its sound was poetry.

I knew that was my last day. My family knew it was my last day. All of my friends and some random strangers I stopped on the street and smooched on the lips knew it was my last day. But my office didn't.

Cruella didn't.

I had been told leaving and never coming back was not the professional approach to quitting, although it sounded the safest. But since the act of abandoning my city job and running away from skyscrapers toward the rolling hills of graduate school felt cowardly, I decided I had to be brave about being a coward. I couldn't quit; I had to formally resign.

My Season of Freedom happened to fall during the 62nd annual Cannes Film Festival, and although the film of our famous person had been denied a spot in the competition, he wasn't taking the hint and insisted on showing his piece de resistunk at some sidebar sideshow. One of the lead actors in the film was supposedly "the new Leonardo DiCaprio." Well, four years later, Leonardo DiCaprio is still Leonardo DiCaprio, and since I can't remember this lead actor's name, I assume he is back to doing video shorts for NYU students.

The good news was that Cruella was to join Famous Guy in the French Riviera for the two-week duration of the festival. The bad news was that her upcoming absence pushed up when I had to submit my resignation.

May 8th. The date that would potentially be engraved on my tombstone.

For the entire week leading up to May 8th, my symptoms read like a Pepto Bismol commercial. And oh, the trembling! Everything from my hands to my bowels to my vocal chords fell victim to an anxiety-induced Parkinson's disease.

Somehow I got through the week, spilling minimal amounts of coffee and guts.

Friday morning I arrived at the office with the crisp resignation letter printed and inserted into a folder, trembling in my hand. I had rehearsed for countless possibilities of Cruella's reaction to my leaving, and was prepared for all but the scenario of her transforming into a She-Hulk and pounding her desk into dust before turning toward me. That one I'd have to play by ear.

But when I walked into our office, I witnessed a warzone. The phone was ringing off the hook, the copy machine was rattling like an automatic weapon, and women were running around screaming. There may have even been chipped nails. I couldn't say for sure. What was obvious was that Cruella was flying to France the next day, and shit needed to get done.

"Nice of you to arrive not a minute before nine. I hope you got plenty of rest. Don't plan on leaving before eight," Cruella said, on her way to the vice president's office. "When I'm done with Anne, you're next."

I slipped my resignation letter into my desk drawer and waited for Cruella's glare to signal that she was ready for me.

Cruella handed me a sheet of paper marked with items and tasks so obscure, I assumed the completion of the scavenger hunt would result in the unveiling of a prize no less valuable than the Holy Grail.

"Well, don't just stare at it. Go," she seethed.

The gun went off and I bolted into the city streets, eyes darting wildly, my resignation letter left behind.

Out of ten bullets, the first three items were:

- International SIM card. One that works.
  (The subtext read, "If I get to France and I can't make a phone call, I will fly back, find you, and force the chip into the smallest orifice on your body. Then I will do the same with the phone itself.)
- Silk stockings. Italian made.
- The following magazines: *Savour*, April; *Traveler*, June; the last three weeks of *Variety*; *Dolce Vita*; *Boxoffice*; *Film Comment*

So the only details I had to figure out on my own so far were: what kind of phone she had; what size stockings she wore; what color she'd prefer; if she wanted sheer, seamed, or control top; which stockings are Italian, and how the hell to purchase back issues of magazines.

Despite the racing of my heart, the tightening in my chest, and the sweat trickling down my back, I had this under control.

No, I didn't. For the second time on the job, I started to cry. Only twice in five months suffering in the eighth circle of Hell. I call that inner strength.

As I wandered up 6th Avenue, tears streaming down my face, snot bubbling out of my nose, and my heart expanding in my throat, I searched for a storefront called, "All the crap Cruella wants for her big stressful trip." But all I could see through my snivels was a damn Famous Ray's Pizza.

"Come on, girlie. Life can't be that bad," a Latino smoking a cigarette said.

If my life was a musical, this is when I'd break out into soprano song and choreographed dance to explain my predicament to this Casanova. He would listen sympathetically and then respond, encouraging me with a soothing tenor and jazz hands. And together (along with some kooky friends we met along the way), we would accomplish my errands with enough spare time to get married in Central Park, a jolly homeless man as the minister.

But, since life is not a musical, I just twisted up my red-splotched face, wiped my nose with my sleeve, and continued on my mournful way.

Even without the help of my belting Latino love interest, I got the job done before sunset. It just took a few frantic texts to my coworkers, running and subwaying all over the city, an angry phone call from Cruella concerning the issue of what the hell was taking me so long, and a pit stop for dollar-a-slice pizza when I felt as if I might faint.

Night of May 8th. Back in the office. Sound the death knell.

I tapped on Cruella's door.

"Can I speak to you for a minute, Cruella?"

"Only if it's of the utmost importance."

Here, I hesitated. She had made it quite clear I wasn't much more than a stain on her day and an extra work expense on her income tax. Perhaps it would only be considerate to let her have some peace and quiet—not to bother her with the inconsequential details of the administrative assistant's departure.

"Well?" she snapped.

Against my better judgment, I entered her office.

"Hi, Cruella. I, I'm sorry to bother you with this, but I'm giving you my two-week notice. Well, th-three-week, actually." *Unless you want me to leave today and never come back. I could never come back.* I dropped the paper on her desk, stretching my arm out to maximize our distance, as if feeding a rabid dog. "Th-thank you so much for the opportunity to work with you." *You've shown me that evil exists.* "I'm grateful." *I've developed a twitch.* "But I unfortunately have decided to go to graduate school." *I'd rather spend $20,000 a year at graduate school than earn $30,000 a year with you in the next room.*

While issuing this memorized speech, I stared at my feet. And stuttered. Porky Pig style. Then I waited. But when Cruella didn't respond, I forced myself to look up, despite the fear that I would find her morphed into a gigantic, green, irradiated, humanoid monster, pulsing with rage.

But she was just Cruella, staring at me in her perpetually annoyed fashion.

"I'm disappointed. You gave us the impression you were interested in this position long-term, so we invested time and money into training you. I feel we were deceived."

"I'm sorry," I said, and braced myself for her eruption.

"You may go," she said and nodded to the door.

I stared at her for a moment, surprised, and maybe even a little dissatisfied with her lack of response. She'd been more volatile at not getting a reservation during restaurant week.

In the end, she wasn't Medusa, the Wicked Witch of the East Side, Satan, or the mutant alter ego of a physicist. She was just a businesswoman, and now that I was no longer her employee, I meant even less to her than I had before.

I was riding the six train on the way back to Grand Central Station. The subway was packed. A group of rowdy teenagers boarded, and they were noticeably on drugs. One of the girls passed out. She fell to the floor, completely unconscious. Everybody looked away, averted their eyes. So did I.

It was time to leave New York City. Whether it was Cruella's fault or my own, I was withdrawing, hiding behind the walls of my exterior, a rat in the corner of herself.

I Hate People, They're the Worst

This segment of I Hate People, They're the Worst is brought to you by The Jerk Who Was Rear-Ended.

It was another beautiful day in the neighborhood: The sound of car horns melded with the music of blaring stereos; the running engines purred idle and anxious like horses at the gate; the grey sky captured the mood of the citizens beneath it; drivers and passengers alike used emphatic body language to express their restlessness and distaste. It was the kind of day and the kind of traffic that would have made Mr. Roger's lean on his horn, roll down his window, and shout, "Would you be f***ing mine, asshole?"

Yup, rush hour on Friday in New York. More specifically, Long Island.

We were driving back from a lovely day spent traipsing around Port Jefferson village, on the six lane "highway" (quotes because highways shouldn't have traffic lights every twenty feet) of route 347 (also called Nesconset Highway, Hauppauge-Port Jefferson Highway, Nesconset-Port Jefferson Highway, or the Smithtown Bypass. Why give a road one name when it can have five? It used to also be called CR 85 and CR 80, but someone decided those extra two names were a bit excessive. Having five names is cool, but seven is a bit much, don't you think?). A red light stopped us at the intersection with Hallock Road, and that's when we witnessed a fender bender.

A red pickup truck was hit from behind, somewhere between the severity of tapped and rear ended, by a black four door sedan, and the driver of the truck bounded from his car.

The man looked like a Steve Buscemi who really let himself go: long, stringy hair; sweat suit ensemble that was probably grease stained; grandpa eyeglasses; and a waist the circumference of an inner tube.

He stormed toward the sedan the way I imagine the giant chased Jack down the beanstalk, and I lowered my window to hear words much more charged than Fee-fi-fo-fum. The adjectives included stupid and a synonym for sexing, the nouns rhymed with witch and hunt. All were repeated multiple times at very high volume, and I can only assume were accompanied by a generous amount of spittle.

The driver of the sedan exited the car, and I could have been looking in the mirror: a woman in her twenties with long dark hair and bookish glasses—a sexy librarian, hold the sexy.

The man, yelling what I now believe to be the only adjectives and nouns in his vocabulary, gestured toward a low platform attached to the back of his truck that carried something covered by a tarp. This is most likely the reason the girl bumped into him; it was probably below her line of vision.

Phil believes the man said, "You killed my sexing pig you sexing witch." But the package didn't appear to be shaped like a hog. I can't rightly say what the mini trailer carried, but from the way the man was reacting, it was either his first-born child or the Ark of the Covenant, although I'm not sure why you'd strap either to the back of your pickup. Then again, from the looks of this guy, Phil could be right—it might have been his prize-winning pig. Which, by all appearances, could have also been his first-born child.

Then the man began slamming his hands on his truck and chanting: Witch. Hunt. Witch. Hunt.

Given that every direction of the four-way

intersection had three lanes, the accident was fairly far away from us. Certainly there were people closer, many directly beside them. I looked into the car windows of the bystanders, and nobody seemed perturbed by the scene. One man examined his cuticles, another bobbed peacefully to music that must have had a beat the tempo of smooth jazz.

I've always admired the heroes featured on the 11 o'clock news who jumped in front of an oncoming subway to save the life of a clumsy stranger. It doesn't happen often, but it happens. The newscaster sticks a microphone in their face and asks, "Weren't you scared? What were you thinking?" and they always answer, "I wasn't thinking, really. It was just instinct." One of the biggest insecurities I have with my character is that, if an emergency strikes, I wouldn't have that instinct to save. I fear my instinct would be to feign fascination with some ceiling beams and, after the all the commotion settles down, I'd shrug and say, "Someone was on the tracks? I had no idea, but have you seen the architecture in this place? Incredible!"

I thought about that as I watched all the surrounding drivers nod to the rhythm of their individual music without showing concern for the wellbeing of their fellow (wo)man. I thought about how I want to be the type of person whose instinct is to jump. To save.

The man stopped pounding his truck and stomped back toward my mirror image. "You stupid hunt!"

"Hey!" I shouted. (Okay, shouted is a misleading verb choice here. It was more like a Neville Longbottom squeal, and I'm not talking Dumbledore's Army Neville. I'm talking round-faced, fell-off-his-broom Neville. Books one and two Neville—pre-puberty, pre-bravery). "Calm down!" Not exactly jumping on the tracks, but at least I wasn't staring at ceiling beams.

The ogre turned slowly and glared in our direction. Yup, I'd definitely angered it. Either he'd heard me, or he'd caught a whiff of something he found particularly unsavory, like carrots or *baked* potato chips. My stomach dropped. I sank a little lower in my seat, pulled my cell phone from my pocket, and dialed 911. Screw the woman on the tracks. This is why we hire a police force. What a waste of our taxpayer money if we don't take advantage of their resources, right?

"Hi, um, we're at the intersection of...Phil, where are we? What are these streets called, again? Oh yeah, Route 347. Yes, Smithtown Bypass. Yes, Nesconset Highway. I can't see the name of the other street, but it's by the Red Lobster. There's been an accident, and the guy who was hit is mean. Like, really mean. He isn't being nice at all."

Our light turned green, so we pulled into the parking lot of the Red Lobster, jumped out of our car, and ran towards the accident. By the time we got there, the truck driver was setting off for a diner across the highway, but the girl still stood beside her sedan, shaken.

"He's crazy!" I yelled. I'm not sure why, it just seemed like the right thing to yell.

"We called the police," Phil said, a much more practical approach.

"Oh, thank you. Well, I guess I better follow him."

Before she could get back into her car, the vehicle behind her honked its horn, pulled down its window, and a woman shouted, "Hey, move it! We don't have all sexing day."

We left the scene then, and although I regretted that my version of a courageous track-jumper turned out to be more high-pitched and timid than I had fantasized, I found solace in the fact that at least I wasn't as bad as that other witch driving behind the accident.

The Crown Jewel

I purchased Jewel tickets with a hint of nostalgia.

Back when gas was cheap enough that you could drive around just for fun, my best friend and I sped down the residential streets of our suburb with the windows down, blasting "Foolish Games." Our hands clasped our hearts, our hair whipped in the wind, and we sang until our throats scratched, thinking, *He* was *fashionably sensitive but too cool to care. How did she know?* And when the song ended, we pressed the back button and let the anguish wash over us again.

I fell asleep to "Break Me" and woke to "Standing Still." Jewel was part of my teenage soundtrack, until I found Emo and became a real, inconsolable wretch.

Now that my parents are no longer out to ruin my life and the world isn't so unfair, Emo is an artifact of my history. I won't touch the stuff. But Jewel? "Who Will Save Your Soul?" "You Were Meant For Me"? "Hands"? There's plenty of space for her music in my present.

So I said, "Oh, by the way, Phil. We're seeing Jewel in concert. Goodnight."

I was a little nervous for Jewel when we arrived at the venue. Ten minutes before the show started, the place was almost empty. I worried the four-time Grammy nominee would walk out onto a stage in nowhere Long Island to serenade only me, Phil, and some guy in a cowboy hat. Phil very generously offered his stomach as a blank canvas on which to draw a message of reassurance. A, "*We're* here for you" or, "It's quality, not quantity," written in borrowed lipstick. But this wasn't necessary because the room filled during the performance of the opener, an acoustic guitar playing country singer with long blonde hair who we suspected was Jewel herself wearing a prosthetic nose, out to catch a sneak-peak of the crowd.

When the opener finished, the stage crew emerged to set up for our headliner. They carried out a table, upon which they placed a bouquet of fresh flowers (classy touch, Jewel) and a packet of papers that Phil guessed to be a collection of lyrics. I joked, "Yeah, because she doesn't know the words to her own songs," and in about 25 minutes, we would learn this to be the case. I guess that's what happens when 20 years have passed since you wrote the damn things. The men lined up three acoustic guitars and one electric, and then sanitized the microphone. Jewel can't know who will save your soul, but she's well aware that Purell is a friend to your immune system.

The theater was sufficiently packed when she walked out, and the crowd rose to their feet to welcome her. One not-effeminate man cupped his hands around his mouth and screamed, "I love you, Jewel!" There were tears in his eyes. These people were my kin.

Jewel parted her lips and took my breath away.

Here's what makes her such a special performer. Inside the span of one song, nay, one line, her vocals metamorphose into very distinct, very separate sounds. There's the whispery resonance, the Mariah Carey-esque belt, the nasal blend, the sweet song, the yodel, and the reverberation—where she wields enough control to sound as if her microphone is echoing inside a coliseum. It's as if she's possessed by the spirits of six singers, blessed with Multiple PersTonality Disorder. The audience gets a handful of artists for the price of one. It's a deal, and I love a deal.

As I gawked at her talents, I couldn't ignore a buzz in my ear.

Two girls at my left shoulder were chatting at great, animated length, as if the concert was the site for their much-anticipated reunion. Perhaps they were twin sisters separated at birth, meeting for the first time, with everything to learn about one another. It's a tender story, and I was happy for them, but take it outside, ladies. I shot them a couple of intentional looks, not necessarily expressing a high level of animosity, because I'm not confrontational, but we made eye contact–enough that, if the tables were turned, it would have registered with me that another concert attendee looked me in the eye while an iconic singer was standing on stage, and since "I" ain't no showstopper, it must be because "I" couldn't SHUT MY DAMN MOUTH. They didn't get the point.

Just as my blood began to boil, the girl closest to me leaned over and actually spoke into MY ear.

"Isn't she amazing?" she asked.

How would you know? I thought, but nodded absently, limiting my response to drive home the point that I was not there to socialize.

"I was disappointed it was standing room only, but she's so amazing I don't mind standing," she said. And when I didn't reply, she prompted me with, "Do you know what I mean?"

I rarely hope that somebody has a mental problem. But in that case, her continual interruption of my experience was so infuriating, I could only forgive her if she was cognitively handicapped.

"Can you save our spots?" she asked then. "We have to go to the bathroom and don't want to lose our spot. We're two people."

I turned toward her, and then looked behind us to confirm that, yes, we still stood at the back of the room, in front of a six square foot empty pocket. There was no need for saving space.

At this point in the show, Jewel had three times asked the audience, in her very cute and funny way, to shut the hell up. I was afraid the pop star might spot

Chatty Cathy and me and assume we were together, that I too was disobeying her repeated requests. This would spoil my chance of one day being best buds with Jewel Kilcher, or as I, her best friend, will call her, JK. In order to get the insistent woman out of my ear, I took a dramatic step to the left to indicate their spots were safe with me.

Then I caught a stale fruity whiff; the undeniable fragrance of cigarettes and hair product. I confirmed this fragrance with another sniff—yes, the woman in front of me was a smoker, and I'm allergic to cigarette smoke. I tried to talk myself off the reaction ledge. *You're fine. This isn't going to affect you because it's diffused in this big open space.* But the roof of my mouth began to itch, and I felt the tingling compulsion to thrust my tongue against it, a motion that produces a throaty quack, a habit my family refers to as "clucking." Sexy, I know.

I was about to ask Phil if we could relocate when Jewel began to sing, "Break Me."

This song is so fragile, so delicate, a pin dropped in the room could shatter it. I hardly allowed myself to breathe, never mind address the irritation inside my mouth. I simply froze. So you can imagine my rage when the man in front of me whispered a joke to his lady, and she responded with an uninhibited snort.

Between the two chatterboxes, the smoker, and the snorter, I'd just about had it with people. I wanted to whisper to Phil, "Duck," and take all my neighbors out with an unforgiving, well-deserved, spinning kick. Only then could I return to appreciate the concert.

Luckily for my peers, I swallowed this impulse. But after Jewel sang the final note of her ballad, I tugged Phil's sleeve and we slid around to a new grouping... where we found Jewel's biggest fan, and that adjective describes both this person's avidity and her size. She was built like a linebacker. She could have worked Jewel's security detail.

Every time this woman cheered Jewel on, which

was often, I jumped. Her voice was so startlingly loud, so sudden and blatant, it was like an air horn. I turned to survey Phil's reaction, and his eyes, too, were widened in fear. We're going to hear her yell, "Yeah, girl!" in our nightmares.

The next song was Jewel's hit, "You Were Meant For Me," which we immediately learned was Big Girl's favorite. She belted along, loud and clear, to the entire song, mistakenly thinking that I paid $50 per ticket to hear *her* sing. Granted, Big Girl's voice was surprisingly pleasant, but still. This wasn't a rock concert. At a folk concert in a small arena, a bellow from a crowd member with this woman's lung capacity was disruptive. I had trouble listening to Jewel over her, and Jewel had a sound system. But I would never have said anything to Big Girl. She could have hammered my head with her fist and pounded me into the ground like in a caveman cartoon.

We left that night with renewed respect for Jewel: for her abilities, her poetic lyrics, her humor, her past (she grew up in a log cabin in Alaska where they survived off the land, and as a teenager lived in her car in CA) and the fact that she is 39 but still looks like a just-discovered 18 year old.

We also left wondering, *is it Long Island people that are obnoxious, or is it just people people?* We've been here so long, it's hard to remember.

Cruising For Chicks

I shouldn't have gotten my driver's license, and everybody knew it. I knew it because, if you are a good driver, the suggestion of a spin around the block shouldn't surge an extreme sport adrenaline rush. My driver's education instructor knew it when she said, "You aren't going to pass. You better wear a low cut shirt to the test." My mother knew it when, on the way to the test, I took a left hand turn into oncoming traffic, thinking I had the right of way just because my light was green.

My poor mother had already been through so much. A few months earlier, she took me out for one of my first drives and was clutching the passenger's door the entire time.

"You're too far right!" she screeched. "You are going to hit a mailbox!"

I rolled my eyes, "Relax, Mom. Stop freaking out. I'm not that bad."

On the way home, I turned too sharply into the driveway and began cruising straight toward a stone pillar. Luckily I had executed the turn at two miles per hour so, although we were heading to our demise, it was only at a crawl.

"Brake!" my mother shrieked. "Brake!"

But I panicked, and couldn't remember which pedal did what. Afraid that I would accidentally press the gas and launch the minivan into the pillar, I did nothing. I couldn't ask my mother to confirm which was which because I was too horrified to speak. So we continued rolling toward the pillar at a cartoonishly slow, but unstoppable pace. All of our muscles clenched as we alternately looked from one another to our stone fate ahead. Our lips parted; from hers escaped a shrill squawk, and from mine a gravelly moan.

Finally, inches from destruction, my terror deepened into clarity. "Which one is the brake?" I asked in a full shout.

"Left! Left!" my mother answered, matching my volume while clinging to her door like an inverted Spiderman.

I imagined two finger L's in my mind, determined which side was left, and slammed on the brakes, literally just in time.

My mother, who'd just learned she agreed to ride in a vehicle controlled by a moron who didn't know which pedal meant go, threw the car into park, ordered me out, stormed around the car to the driver's side, and drove the rest of the way down the driveway, leaving me beside the pillar to think about what I'd done.

She enrolled me in driver's education the next day, deciding I should learn with someone who had access to their own brake.

But except for a fictional video about a young driver who kills a highway construction worker, which, though poorly produced, still chills me to this day, driver's education had little effect on my skills—or lack thereof. The woman who conducted the classroom was a smoker with a husky, diner waitress voice, who spent most of the 45 minute sessions flirting with boys a third of her age. The oversized man who escorted me on road hours missed his calling to be Randy Jackson, and dedicated most of our road time to belting along with his Bonnie Raitt CD, so much so that, while his eyes were closed, head tilted back, and mouth agape, he missed me assume green means go, making a left turn into oncoming traffic. The honks of angry drivers were barely audible over the emotionally charged lyrics, *And I will give up this fight!* Proving you can go both Raitt *and* left.

And so, I never learned rights of way and made the same mistake on the day of the driver's test, with my mother in the passenger seat. She concluded, not irrationally, that driver's education was a complete waste of money, and I would surely fail the test.

The test was administered at the driver's education school, by a visiting DMV proctor. I sat in a room with a handful of other nervous sixteen year olds and watched as, one by one, we were selected to go out on the road. And, one by one, they returned. Some shaken, some near tears, all having failed.

A scrawny teen who I shared a couple road hours with came back with an ashen face. "Our driver's ed instructor told me not to worry. He was sure I'd pass," he whispered to no one. "Sure of it," he repeated, even quieter.

The smoker driver's ed instructor walked over and patted Scrawny Teen's back. "It isn't your fault," she said. "The proctor got a speeding ticket this morning. He's in a mood and failing everyone." Then she made eye contact with me, lowered her eyes to my chest, resumed eye contact, and raised her eyebrows in an expression that said, *It's your only hope.* I swallowed hard while Smokey's back pats continued lower and lower down Scrawny Teen's back. His day was getting worse by the second.

My hands were trembling by the time it was my turn. I followed the proctor out into the parking lot and glanced down at my front. *You're better than that,* I told myself. But the truth was, when it came to driving, I wasn't better. I was bad. A liability, even. I gave my shirt hem a tug.

I sat in the driver's seat and greeted the proctor. Then I shifted the car into gear, turned to look behind me, released the brake, and, as my mind and body anticipated the vehicle's gentle backward glide, the car lurched forward and bashed into a chain link fence. I had not put the car in reverse. I had put it in drive. A horribly stupid mistake, but not a surprising one for me.

At this point, I figured I might as well just get out of the car, wish the proctor good day, and go our separate ways. No need to waste either of our times with the formality of finishing the exam; I'd obviously already failed. How many people can pass a driver's test after crashing the car?

"Take a deep breath. You're obviously just very nervous. Let's start over," the man said.

What had just happened? Did the low cut shirt actually work? I looked down at myself. No, the Dillons were late bloomers—it wasn't the shirt. My error was just too garish to take seriously; he assumed it was nerves—not incompetence. He didn't know I sometimes forgot which pedal was which. He didn't know I wasn't so clear on those pesky right of way details. He assumed I could be a fine driver who flubbed.

"Yes, I'm just nervous," I said, nodding. "I definitely know that drive means forward."

So I began again. And, miracle of miracles, I passed. I'm not sure how, I don't remember a thing about the rest of the test. To compensate for that initial blunder, the spirit of Dale Earnhardt must have possessed me. (Dale Earnhardt is the name I found when I googled "famous racecar driver dead." For the purposes of this paragraph, let's ignore the fact that he died in a car crash.)

I emerged from that test with the sloppy grin of a person who had just gotten lucky. I walked into the room of sixteen year olds and said, "I passed!"

The skinny teen from earlier, who was still there and still pale, said, "You're kidding me. *You* passed? Everybody was sure you of all people would fail."

It was obvious I wasn't going to find enthusiasm for my accomplishments in a room full of non-licensed duds, so I continued out of the building to meet my mother. On the way out, I heard the teen ranting, "This is ridiculous. *She* passes and *I* fail?"

I saw my mother waiting, looking as if she was still peeved from when my little error in judgment almost cost her life. But my good tidings of great joy were sure to brighten her mood.

"I passed!" I said with arms outstretched. Bring on the merriment.

"The state of Connecticut might be stupid, but I'm not," she said and got in the car on the driver's side, leaving my still open arms empty.

You put a person in direct peril for just a couple of seconds and they stew about it all day. Mothers.

Well, the woman had a point. Having a license in my wallet did not improve my skills.

First, I backed into a brick wall—but, in my defense, I hit it lightly. I'd cruised down the narrow driveway of a storefront that looped behind the building and then just ended. If I didn't want to sit there with the engine running until I died of exhaust fumes or starvation, I'd have to retrace my route. Well, I didn't feel comfortable reversing out. I was really more of a forward-moving driver. So I made a three-point turn that, in the limited square of that back alley, became a thirty-point turn. I rolled forward an inch, hit the curb, shifted into reverse, turned the wheel, rolled back an inch, shifted into drive, turned the wheel, and repeated—thirty times. The entire enterprise took about ten minutes to complete. That scene from *Austin Powers: International Man of Mystery* with the luggage cart in the hallway hits a little too close to home. Well, on one of the moves I was a bit too daring in my reverse and may have kind of plowed into the building. Paint was scraped from the rear in brick sized stripes— defacement I would feign ignorance of later.

Second, I backed into a friend's car with enough force to imprint a bumper shaped ditch above her front wheel. That's the day I learned, when you're backing out of your garage, check behind you first. My friend did not freak out, at least not openly. And, bless her and her parents' hearts, they allowed me to pay them for the damage in installments dropped into their mailbox on the first Monday of every month, organized-crime style. I managed this secret payoff by teaching piano to neighborhood kids—at least one of whom knew she was better than me; I saw glint of pity in her eye—and by making a phone call to the most compassionate man in my contacts: my grandpa. He padded my high school graduation check with a little extra so my parents weren't the wiser, and every time he saw me for the next couple of years would greet me and then whisper something cheeky like, "Any more games of bumper cars?"

To top it all off, I jumped a few curbs. Some so badly that I tore holes in the tires. But, come on, who doesn't do that?

Then, the inevitable: I totaled the family minivan—the same car that had survived all my previous scuffles. That dear green Chrysler Town and Country with the drop-down television and the automatic closing door was crushed before its time. It still had many good miles left. But after the first close encounter with the stone pillar, I'm sure the minivan saw this coming long ago, and viewed every day it safely returned to the garage as an unexpected gift.

One January morning, there was a snow and ice storm severe enough to delay school districts across Connecticut. My mother came back from walking the dog, limping, because she had fallen on ice.

"Drive carefully. It's really slick out there," she said.

"Yeah, okay," I said.

Well, you can guess the end of this story. I severely underestimated the dangers of icy conditions.

You know how they say that when you hit a patch of ice, you should turn into the skid? Well, I'm happy to say that I retained the presence of mind to know that I would certainly screw that up. So, instead, I threw my hands in the air and let Jesus take the wheel. I know they didn't have cars back in his day, but even as a first time driver I knew he'd make a smoother recovery than me.

I spun. And I think I spun again. A telephone pole stopped me. I bounced off it and landed facing the wrong direction.

I panted for several breaths. My entire body pulsed. I looked down. My arms were crossed over my chest. Perhaps hugging yourself and screaming isn't the most strategic defense when a vehicle loses control but, no matter—I was alive!

Then, maybe from watching *Bad Boys* too many times, I became convinced that the rattled engine was seconds from combusting. I turned off the ignition, abandoned the vehicle, and ran. When I gained enough distance, I faced my poor crumpled vehicle and prepared for fireworks.

A man ran out of his house in his bathrobe and slippers, startled, most likely, by the apocalyptic collision noises.

"Are you all right?" he asked.

I nodded. "Don't worry. I turned the car off. It shouldn't explode."

"I'll call the police," he said, and probably because I looked and sounded unstable, added, "And an ambulance."

I called my house. My mom answered and I broke into sobs, crying for both the trauma that transpired and the trauma I anticipated.

When my parents stepped out of their car, I ran toward them.

My dad hugged me, looked up at the shriveled metal that used to cart his family around town, and said, "And I'd just filled up the gas tank."

For weeks I expected punishment, but it never arrived. Maybe my parents thought the experience was consequence enough, or maybe they were too grateful for the consequence they themselves narrowly avoided to enforce one of their own.

The neighborhood of my crash site lost power for

days. And we had to pay $3,000 for the pole, which, in my opinion, was a bunch of bull cocky because the poles on that block were black with rot. It was probably about to fall over anyway.

The car and my reputation were crushed that day, but at least the car could be sold for parts. Which parts? Well, I'm pretty sure the back bumper was in decent condition—save for the scratches from backing into the brick wall. My reputation as a driver on the other hand was a total, complete loss.

The Hitchhiker's Guide To Getting To The Festival His Own Damn Self

The hitchhiker sat in my backseat and, staring back at him, I couldn't make sense of how he got there.

I was sixteen: new to SAT prep, reported income, and the driver's seat of a car. What I wasn't new to was Fairfield, Connecticut—my hometown. And yet I found myself lost, roaming the windy, startlingly unfamiliar streets, no more than five miles from my house.

My friend and I were on our way to the Dogwood Festival, an annual fair at which area vendors gathered on a church green to sell homemade soaps, potted chrysanthemums, and organic dog treats. It doesn't sound like the most stimulating weekend activity for a couple of teenagers, but this was a town whose young people frequently convened in empty fields to stare at one another and drink cheap beer, so at least that day's field would have crafts to admire, and fewer puddles of vomit to sidestep.

The trick, it turned out, was getting there. I'd left the house assuming I knew the way. How could I not? What human of moderate intelligence couldn't retrace a route taken at least a dozen times before? Even rats managed to navigate a maze if it yielded a cheese reward, and that's regular store-bought Kraft cheddar. The Dogwood Festival hosted cheese artisans—I'm talking fresh chevre! But there I was, driving in circles.

This was an age before GPS's, and when cell

phones could only be used to call, text, or bludgeon home invaders. So when I saw a man on the side of the road—a kind soul who could potentially point me in the right direction—I was so relieved, I pulled over without minding his worn duffel bag or the fact that we were in the woods and there was no good reason to trust a man walking along the side of the road. And yet there I was, pulled up beside him, rolling down my window.

"Excuse me, sir. Do you know how to get to the Dogwood Festival?"

Now, this fair was a nice enough event, but Fairfield is a town of 60,000, and the Dogwood Festival wasn't exactly its equivalent to New York City's Puerto Rican Day Parade or Whoville's Christmas. Sure, some people knew about it, and maybe a few even looked forward to it, but it's not like a stranger taken at random would respond to my question with, "The Dogwood Festival? Golly, I surely do know the way! Let me draw you a map." The more likely response would be, "The Dogwood Festival? Um, sounds familiar. I think my cousin's neighbor bought his mom a plant for Mother's Day there once."

But this man—who in my exaggerated memory looked like a young Jerry Garcia, but in reality was likely cleaner, say an older John Lennon—looked at me and said, "Yes, that's where I'm going."

And then he was in my backseat, door shut behind him, and I can't remember how he got from point A to point B.

I turned and stared back at the stranger in my car for an uncomfortable amount of time, long enough to consider many thoughts, the first being, *Is this a big deal?* I try to avoid being dramatic and, when you're inside the moment, it's often hard to measure significance. It's only later, when you're chained up in an unfinished basement, that you realize, *Yup, that was a big deal.*

I then contemplated that the man could be good: a weary traveler, journeying from a far distance—

Woodstock, New York would be a safe guesstimate—to haggle with the artists of New England over one-of-a-kind stuff, like say a hand painted spoon rest, to keep in his duffel bag. Or perhaps he was a craftsman himself, eager to peddle the coasters he'd constructed from littered bottle caps. But then there were other possibilities to ponder, the least gruesome being auto theft, and after a month of driving our Chrysler Town and Country to school, I just couldn't go back to taking the bus.

So at this point in my baffled stare, I arrived at the conclusion that I needed to remove this vagabond from my minivan. The question was, how?

An eject switch, a little red button beneath my dashboard illustrated with a stick figure flung from a vehicle, would have been the ideal solution. However, this was the year 2004, not an episode of *Get Smart*. Back to the drawing board. My next idea was a simple one: ask him to leave. But that felt rude, and I didn't want to seem like some privileged white girl from the suburbs who thought she was too good to give a hobo a lift—we were going to the same place, for crying out loud! So, like I was taught to do when I didn't want to go to a classmate's birthday party, I told a little white lie to spare the vagrant's feelings.

"Actually we have to stop and pick up a friend first, so you probably want to head there on your own," I said, and sighed relief in the wake of my own socially conscious brilliance.

"Oh, I'll come along. I don't mind the stop," he said.

"Oh you don't mind the stop? That's good, that's good," I said, my head bobbing as if trying to physically shake an excuse loose in my brain. "Well, here's the thing though. We may not even go to the festival. I was just asking directions out of curiosity. But what we're doing is stopping at a friend's house, and then, only at that point, are we going to decide. We may go, but we may not. And the second part, the part about not going, is a strong possibility. Getting stronger by the minute, actually. So just get out of my car because out of my car you can go to the festival and be out of my car."

God bless the drifter, he did, and he took his dingy duffel bag with him. As I peeled away, I looked into my rearview mirror; the dust from my quick exodus settled and revealed a harmless nomad, shoulders rounded with fatigue, worn by his pilgrimage, just a guy hoping for a ride.

But at least he knew where he was going.

Ice Cream Cones, And Other Small Stuff Not To Sweat

I'd been waiting all winter for the weather to warm—anticipating, conceptualizing, obsessing over vanilla soft serve ice cream cones with rainbow sprinkles. All three years we'd lived in our apartment, a Carvel sat within walking distance, and I never knew. But now I knew, and the ghosts of unlicked cones haunted me. I watched the second hand tick toward spring, and as soon as the chilled air receded into the ground I was panting at our front door like a Labrador with a full bladder.

We walked to Carvel. Who am I kidding? I skipped. And every piece of normally dismal looking scenery—lawn ornaments in the form of plastic deer and rusty hubcaps, houses lined up hip to hip, the crazy shirtless guy on the corner—were all buffed and burnished with a cheerful gloss. I wasn't even that embarrassed when two children waved and I returned their salute with an enthusiastic gesture and a peppy, "Hey there!", only to realize they were greeting the man behind me—their father—and I was just the weird neighborhood lady who cooed at strange children. Phil comforted my ego with the promise of later taunting those unfriendly runts with our Carvel delicacies.

And then I saw it: Carvel—the sugared cream mecca—trumped only by the monarchical Dairy Queen and the mythical home soft serve machine. I quickened my step and looked past the dirty storefront into the heaven within.

I recited my order to the angelic middle-aged Asian woman behind the counter wearing the blue collared Carvel t-shirt and white company visor. As she pulled ice cream from the machine, expertly rotating her cone wrist to catch the soft serve pouring forth, she looked more appealing than an Oktoberfest Fraulein at a beer tap.

The cone was perfect, the soft serve beginning wide at the base, ripples trailing round and round up to the summit, climaxing into an artfully swirled pinnacle. The rainbow sprinklings speckled its face like unnaturally colored autumn leaves on a Vermont mountain.

And the taste was just as sublime. Absolute bliss. Dairy dessert rapture. Not the icy crap that some establishments shamelessly call soft serve (ahem, Baskin Robbins). But the thick, sweet, cream I would gladly replace my saliva with if I was given three wishes. (The first two are between the genie and me.)

Sometimes when you go a while without tasting something you enjoy, you place the experience on a pedestal, and after so much build-up, it's ultimately a disappointment. But not that cone. That cone was everything I'd idealized it to be.

The Carvel woman rang up our two small cones as I floated on a cloud of euphoria.

"$9.45," she said, and my high came crashing down, landing flat-faced on the intersection between my unsettling passion for soft serve and my frugality. It was an ugly place.

Ten bucks for two small cones? Ten freaking bucks? I didn't remember it being that expensive. How much time had passed since the last ice cream season? A *Game of Thrones* winter? For the price of two small Carvel cones, I could have stocked my freezer with four 1.5 quart cartons of on-sale Edy's—that is if my freezer wasn't too small to hold the sheer volume of ice cream that ten dollars could buy.

A couple ice cream cones heavier and ten bucks lighter, we left the establishment. On the way out, I spotted a flyer on the window: "Soft serve ice cream sundaes: buy one get one free—today only!"

I had been so excited to get in and score my much anticipated cone, I'd rushed by a promo advertisement that would have gotten us twice the ice cream for half the cost. Oh cruel world!

Well, there's no point stewing in it, I told myself. *It's over. Nothing you can do. Let it go and enjoy your ice cream. You sure paid enough for it.* But I couldn't shake the idea that I'd been ripped off, and that I'd missed out on a deal. I'd spent years training my eye to spot bargains. Years. *You're better than that, Dillon!* I thought, and from that point on, every delicious lick was undermined by a bitter aftertaste—the flavor of loss.

I was so bummed, I didn't even flaunt my yummy acquisition to those scuzzy little lawn brats who couldn't bother to say hello to me.

Phil and I finished our Ice Cream For The Rich And Famous about a block from our house. I offered to take Phil's cone wrapper because I'm a generous wife, and because I'd convinced him to let me have his last bite, and holding his trash until we reached our garbage seemed a reasonable courtesy tax.

I was beginning to mentally draft an angry missive to the corporate ice cream dictators when the wind picked up, and Phil's paper wrapper escaped my fingertips.

It scurried down the sidewalk, flitted onto a neighbor's lawn, and returned to the sidewalk, performing a jaunty dance like the chimney sweep in *Mary Poppins*. I chased after it, and I am not a graceful chaser. Just as I plodded my foot down in its vicinity, it skidded to the right and narrowly avoided my toe. It was as if the wrapper was attached to an invisible string, and a higher power mistook me for a cartoon cat, tugging it out of reach just as I was about to grab it. I stomped and failed three times before finally bearing down on my target. With the wrapper finally underfoot, I bent over to retrieve it, but lifted my shoe seconds before my fingers had secured a grip. The wrapper broke away and again fled down the street. I jogged after it, and had to increase my speed to a full on sprint to catch up. When it was again within my grasp, I lurched forward, my hand propelling ahead with vigor and determination. I punched the sidewalk. The skin on my knuckles scraped away, but I had the wrapper.

I spun around, victorious, lifting the wrapper high like a Spartan warrior brandishing an enemy's decapitated head, (blood dripping down in both scenarios), only to find Phil buckled over, cackling. I'm talking literal knee slapping. And across the lawn to my "husband's" right, an elderly gentleman sat on his porch in a rocking chair, also chuckling at the post-cone klutz who was nearly outwitted by a piece of paper.

Then I looked down at myself—at the woman who waited months for her ice cream cone and then fumed over its cost through the duration of its consumption. I'd taken soft serve, an Alexander Hamilton-themed bill, and myself way too seriously, and ended up racing Stooge-like behind a wrapper.

And then I too got the joke, and laughed.

Wedding Crashers

I went to two weddings on a recent Saturday, only one of which I was invited to.

The first wedding, celebrating my husband's childhood friend and his beautiful bride, was wonderful, and I had a table card with my name on it. The food was tasty, the champagne bubbly, and the live band piqued my appetite for grooving.

I am not a great dancer, but I am an enthusiastic one. People who know me might say, "Hey, you were on the dance team in high school so you can't be that bad!" But I would remind those people that our dance team placed last in all statewide competitions (go Mustangs!), and that I shouldn't have made that worst-in-Connecticut team in the first place.

During tryouts, as we performed before judges in groups of four, I jumped ahead in the choreography, and the other three dancers, all of whom were better than me, followed along, perhaps realizing that as a unit we'd look silly having one odd duck strutting to her own beat. Because of my misstep, we struck our final pose a good five seconds before the song ended. As we awkwardly froze in dead space, waiting for the music to end, I said, "Well this can't be good." The judges laughed, and I made the team—not for my rhythm, but for my comedic timing. Later, the team captain reinforced this idea with constructive criticism like, "I don't know how you made this team. You move like a Tyrannosaurs Rex." And in case her language wasn't vivid enough, she demonstrated what she meant with a pretty decent dinosaur impression while the rest of the team snickered.

Anyway, back to the weddings. Like all great receptions, this one ended too soon. It's strange how when you fill a room with steak, cake, booze, and music, time is warped and five hours feels like five minutes.

After the reception, we left the hall and continued the party back at the hotel bar. This hotel happened to be hosting another wedding. And their band sounded really good. My boogie hunger growled.

I was able to suppress my freshly tantalized cravings until the band broke out into a romping rendition of perennial wedding favorite, "Shout." To fully understand why I couldn't possibly resist this Isley Brother hit, kindly join me on a tangent. You won't be sorry.

Wind chimes to cue flashback

Phil and I landed a kick ass band for our wedding. They called themselves, No Big Deal, but it was an ironic name because they knew they were at least kind of a big deal. We sat in on one of their practices before we hired them, to ensure that they were as good as their online sound bites suggested. Their Gigmasters profile didn't do justice to their live performance. As they crooned through reception favorites such as, "At Last," "The Way You Look Tonight," and "You Give Love A Bad Name," my eyes watered.

"Do you play 'Sweet Caroline'?" I asked. My dad is a Neil Diamond nut, and my paternal family sang "Sweet Caroline" before it was a popular bar hit. I insist we were the first to flavor the song with its signature *Bah, bah-bah!*'s, although Phil contends with equal fervor that it isn't true.

"We do play 'Sweet Caroline'," they answered.

"This is the band," I said, my voice cracking. "This is the band."

On the big day, No Big Deal was phenomenal. They flawlessly transformed their sound testing into a premature cocktail hour jazz session when all of the guests arrived an hour early because I screwed up the timing of the ceremony. Sure the lead singer mispronounced my name when introducing us, but who doesn't mispronounce my name? The vowels are tossed in there so arbitrarily, sometimes I even get confused.

The band owned the crowd that night. As per our request, they avoided pretty much any "music" released after the turn of the millennium (with the exceptions of John Mayer and early Maroon 5, before they lost their way mingling with the likes of Christina Aguilera). My use of quotations there is obvious but, for fans of auto-tune, I think we use the word "music" a little fast and loose when referring to a lot of the machine generated compositions on the radio today. And yes, I just heard that I sound like a grumpy senior citizen.

I jumped around so fervently to artists like Bon Jovi and The Rolling Stones that I stretched out my ivory satin wedding dress and had to be wary of rocking it right to the floor. I knew my guests were having a great time too when the band tried to slow it down with "What A Wonderful World," and they booed. I'd judge everybody for being so rude, except that I was their leader.

Then, out of nowhere, it was over. Damn the curse of the wedding time warp.

"Last song!" the singer announced. We responded with more wild boos.

My younger brother, who was dripping with sweat that was mostly top-shelf vodka and wearing sunglasses with only one lens, grabbed my shoulder.

"It better be 'Shout,'" Ryan said. For months leading up to the wedding, Ryan had been advocating that "Shout" is the ultimate wedding song, and declared it a mandatory feature during our celebration. I agreed, but with less passion.

It wasn't "Shout." It was Led Zeppelin's "Rock n' Roll." And we pumped our fists until the final note.

"Thank you everybody. You've been a great

crowd!" The singer said.

"One more song, one more song," we chanted, as is customary, certain there was an encore coming. They couldn't just cut us off when we were so obviously in want of more jams. But when the singer stuck her microphone in its stand and turned to gather her things, we realized that, apparently, they could.

After all the anticipation leading up to our wedding—all of the Google searches, price comparisons, venue viewing, hotel reservations, dress fittings, invitation selecting, envelope addressing, RSVP counting, seating chart building, hair trialing, bouquet arranging, and ice cream sacrificing—and after all the decisions: Which hymns? Which readings? Do we give a hoot about favors? Should we hire a videographer or ask a cousin to film because we probably will never watch it anyway? Flower centerpieces or petals and votive candles? White or ivory? Is swing dancing too flippant for a first dance? Heels or flats? Band or DJ? Buffet or sit down? Elope now or just get drunk and stick it out?—it was hard to believe that the night was finished. Recent bride cousins had cautioned me to savor every moment because the day would fly by. And I did. I don't think I spoke to anybody who didn't meet me on the dance floor, but now I had danced my last dance. Tens of thousands of dollars spent, and now the night was over. Tragic, but true. I had to accept reality. I turned to say goodbye to one of my guests when—

"Now wa-a-a-a-it a minute!"

This was not the female singer of No Big Deal. This was a male voice. I spun around. It was my little brother, Ryan, hair soaked with perspiration, jacket and vest discarded, tie askew, sleeves rolled up, shirt half tucked and water stained, still wearing the sunglasses with one lens. And holding the band's microphone.

Ryan was all confidence, as if his entire life was preparing him for this moment. But I froze, teetering on the triangular brink of mortification, dread, and excitement.

The band made us sign a contract promising none of our guests would touch their equipment. At the time, the idea of it made us giggle. We imagined our friends storming the stage, grabbing their instruments in a musical coup d'etat. "You know that must have happened at one of their other wedding gigs. Some wasted guest must have thought he was a rock star," we'd said, laughing heartily, and then signed the contract without hesitation, assuming it was a meaningless formality.

"You know you make me want to shout!" Ryan sang.

The band stared at Ryan, surely not knowing how to react. But the crowd knew what to do. They jumped. They pumped. I joined in, figuring if we were going to pay for it, I might as well enjoy it, and by god, we shouted.

"Throw your hands up and shout, throw your head back and shout. Come on now!"

This is when Ryan realized that he knew the beginning of the song, and he knew the end of the song, but there was a chunk in the middle that escaped him. No matter. He wasn't going to let such an insignificant detail as lyrics dull his spotlight. He skipped on to the end.

"A little bit softer now, a little bit softer now, a little bit softer now," Ryan commanded, and we all obeyed, our voices softening, twisting low until we were crouching near the ground.

"A little bit louder now, a little bit louder now," Ryan continued.

At this point, the band looked silly just standing by, idly doing nothing, so the guitarists picked up their instruments and joined in. Ryan got so excited by this new development in his act that he lost his rhythm, and we all had to coach him back on track until—

"HEY-EY-EY-EY!"

For the last chorus, the lead singer reclaimed her microphone and shooed Ryan off the stage. But it was because of him that we had that extra final moment, and I think he'd want me to share that, for his courage, some have called him The Party Hero.

Wind chimes to signal transition back into the recent weekend's wedding(s)

So, in the hotel bar, a year and a half after our wedding, the first few notes of "Shout" triggered a precious memory, and I could not ignore the call to action. I cinched up my floor length dress (my high heels had long since been kicked off) and sprinted toward the source of nostalgia. Phil, a devoted fan of 60's R&B and of yours truly, didn't miss a beat. We even inspired one of Phil's childhood friends to join the cause. We all ran down the hall, into the reception room, possessed by Vince Vaughn and Owen Wilson characters, and didn't stop until we were on the dance floor, amidst the other guests, throwing our heads back and Shout!ing.

Nobody said anything. Nobody else seemed to be aware of an intrusion. They just smiled at us and nodded an appreciation for our "Shout" fervor. And we were fervent. Our hands waved like African priests seized by spirits.

Perhaps we should have left when the song ended. Or the one after. Or the one after that. Perhaps I shouldn't have made my way to the front of the dance floor to mirror the very soulful lead singer. Perhaps we shouldn't have stayed for the rest of the wedding, including the heartwarming number, Sister Sledge's "We Are Family," in which we sang along and spread our arms out to address the entire room of strangers. Perhaps we shouldn't have kissed the bride on the lips. But we did. Okay, not the last one, but the rest are true.

But we didn't drink their booze, or eat their cake. We just shared their joy, and maybe added a little of our own. So perhaps it's they who should thank us, for doing our part to make their celebration as special as it was. And perhaps it's Ryan I should thank for the, albeit unconventional, marital memory he created, which will forever be triggered by "Shout," and instill new meaning in the lyrics: *I still remember...*

One Shouldn't Snort at the Waldorf

When the Waldorf Astoria Hotel popped up on Priceline's page, I had to rub my eyes and look again like a cartoon's depiction of disbelief.

Priceline's Name Your Own Price feature works like this. You set your parameters: neighborhood, star rating, and price. Then you press submit and Priceline books any hotel that agrees to your terms. My terms were low, so I expected to spend our getaway in New York City at a per night crack den.

Thanks to some miracle glitch, Priceline upgraded us to a room at the Waldorf Astoria. How do Phil and I feel about reaching the height of fanciness at the ripe ages of 25 and 29? We feel great.

Leading up to the stay, we were giddy with anticipation:

"Should I get my haircut?" Phil asked the night before.

"No, leave it shaggy. People will think we must be famous to look so disheveled at The Waldorf."

"Check my teeth," I said, a block away from the hotel. "I can't have anything in my teeth at The Waldorf."

As 49th Street met Park Avenue, we stopped and gazed at its gold-leafed entrance with the type of reverence we usually reserve for that initial moment when you open a pizza box and the steam pours forth.

"Valet parking," I whispered, like a prayer, not that we even had a car to park.

We pushed through the revolving doors (which were also gold—I was starting to think the hotel architect was Scrooge McDuck) and walked through the Park Avenue lobby, slowly, gazing up at the ornate molding, chandeliers, and frescoes of Romans or Greeks enjoying themselves (they live at The Waldorf, so of course they were enjoying themselves).

There are multiple lobbies at The Waldorf. The Park Avenue lobby was originally designed so that women could wait there while their husbands paid the bills because, at the time, it was considered inappropriate for females to witness the exchange of money. I suppose not too much has changed in this case because, although I paid for the room, Priceline and Visa protected me from the dirty dealings.

We followed the mosaic-tiled floor and passed chinchilla fur coats, meeting rooms named after oil tycoons, and not one, not two, but three grand pianos, until finally arriving at the crown jewel.

The main lobby of The Waldorf looked as if Grand Central Station and The Palace of Versailles drank a little too much Dom Perignon one night and conceived a bouncing baby hotel, complete with plush carpeting, pillars, and a 9-foot, two-ton bronze clock. While we waited in line in the bustling lobby that was dripping with elegance, Phil read the clock placard and remarked, "It was commissioned the year I was born." The placard date read 1893, but Phil reversed the middle two numbers in his mind. Innocent mistake, I know, but the idea of Phil claiming to be 119 years old made me snort-laugh, which made me elbow Phil for causing me to snort-laugh in the main lobby of The Waldorf.

If there was anybody who looked more out of place than me in the landmark hotel, it was Phil, a man who, as a graduate student, took tours of abandoned undergraduate dorms and pillaged the stuff (dishes, notepads, extension cords, socks) left behind. So he took great pleasure watching me attempt to camouflage my pig sound under a hearty throat clear, while women in diamonds and chinchilla—accessories worn only by WASPS and rappers—wondered when The Waldorf opened their doors to peasants.

After a few minutes in line, as I pondered that a salad with walnuts and grapes—two decadent food items that are often too expensive for us to buy—was named after this living museum, a uniformed bellhop with gold tasseled shoulder pads escorted us to the next available receptionist.

"Reservation for Dillon," I said with a proud smile. The lady nodded and clicked her keyboard.

"All right, it says here that the room is prepaid through Priceline?" she asked.

She said it perfectly nicely, without a hint of judgment, but this was The Waldorf, and I knew she was just being polite. It took every ounce of my self-discipline not to shush her.

She issued us our room keycards, which had to be used to access the elevators, and we bumbled onward, still in awe of our surroundings, trying not to look like the Beverly Hillbillies, or the Wald-Oafs.

The wonder continued in our room, which had a doorbell that I rang only three times. I stood in the bathroom, a luxurious little world of white marble, and was disappointed by a smudge on the mirror. As I rubbed the discoloration to remove it, the area flashed, and the local news came on. It was a television. Embedded. Inside. The. Mirror.

"Phil, Phil!" I screeched, shaking my hands like a child who doesn't know how to express excitement. He peeked his head around the corner, seemed frightened for a moment, and then approached the image with the apprehensive curiosity of a dog navigating a vacuum. He looked around the room, attempting to identify the source of this moving picture. Then he waved his hand in front of it, presuming it was projected.

"No, it's coming from inside," I said, sounding more like a cavewoman discovering fire than a guest at a historic luxury hotel.

The Waldorf insignia radiated gold on every surface. It was emblazoned on the soap, robes, and pillows—even on the toilet paper. I imagined that, right before we arrived, a man in a tuxedo patrolled the room carrying The Waldorf stamper, and branded every object that had an edge.

In the main area of the room, I approached the desk and opened a thick leather portfolio, revealing an extensive display of Waldorf stationery (cards and card envelopes, paper and letter-sized envelopes, postcards). I read online that every President since Herbert Hoover has enjoyed these lush accommodations. As I admired the regal selection of writing materials, I envisioned a President of the United States sitting at that mahogany desk, composing an important correspondence on the thick linen paper (which of course glittered with the golden Waldorf insignia). I sighed at the beauty of this image, and then stuffed the stationery in my purse.

After surveying the room, we flopped down on the Italian linens, read the Guest Directory, and learned some very important facts about The Waldorf. For instance, after 6 pm the hotel kindly requested a business casual dress code in the lobbies. Since Phil and I were wearing jeans, and didn't bring a change of pants, we would be kindly declining that request. Also, there weren't ice machines on the floor. Ice was delivered to the room and, a few hours later, we would learn that it was literally brought on a silver platter. Lastly, every Friday and Saturday night at 7 pm, The Waldorf offered a magic show by Steve Cohen, The Millionaires' Magician. However, if the time was not convenient, Mr. Cohen was also available for private in-suite appearances. I pictured a wealthy couple with a previous engagement at 7 pm, sitting on their bed after their jaunt about town, wearing ballroom attire, looking severely unimpressed while The Millionaires' Magician pulled the 2012 Best In Show prize-winning toy poodle out of his top hat.

That night, we slept in an official New York landmark—which is even cooler than when I peed at the New York Public Library. Now I just have to decide which of my family or friends is deserving of a note on Waldorf letterhead.

It Came To Pass That I Am Not Great With Children

I've officially arrived at that time in my life when, recently married and surrounded by family members in the baby-making business, I'm fielding inquiries about my personal procreation timeline. (This includes family planning questions from my gynecologist, who was accused of fertilizing one of his patients with his own sperm, so my adamant head shakes at him were for slightly different reasons. You're probably wondering why this criminal is still my gynecologist, as most of my family and friends do, and the answer is that he's just so convenient. It isn't every doctor you can call at the last minute and still have your pick of appointments. Rest assured, as soon as I *am* ready to think about motherhood, I'm getting the hell out of there.)

I'm not eager for offspring, at least not any time soon. In addition to the major concern—that having a child means that I'll... have a child—there is another factor staining the vision of me as a mother, and that is the memory of me as a babysitter.

Before I divulge further details, I'd first like to issue the disclaimer that I am very good with kids, and generally really enjoy them. The problem is, even the best kids are not well behaved all the time. I have A LOT of babysitting experience: over ten years of regularly sitting and/or nannying. So, there were moments when great kids were bad, and when a good babysitter was worse.

This is my story...

Part I

It was a hot summer, and most high school girls in Fairfield County spent their days at the beach or poolside, leeching off their richer friends' country club memberships. But I didn't have access to a car, spare cash, or leisure time, because I had totaled the family minivan against the south side of a telephone pole four months earlier. Thus, I was sentenced to a summer of strapping on a neon helmet and bike riding to my full-time nannying gig, where I was expected to design activities to entertain two very reluctantly entertained young boys for eight hours a day. They were the kind of boys who liked to say, "I'm bored. There's nothing to do," and "No, I don't want to do that. That's stupid," and then, when they finally did come up with a game to play, it involved hitting each other with weapon-shaped objects.

It was the end of August and I was tired, and the boys were tired of hearing me say things like, "Stop doing that," and "Get your finger out of his nose," and "Running through the woods with your eyes closed isn't the best idea if you ever want to turn seven."

On one fateful morning, I decided it'd be fun to take the boys to the lake. In my naivety, I urged them to change into swimsuits and get their beach gear together. The elder boy complied, but the younger boy, who was too young to be officially diagnosed with ADD but would surely see Ritalin in his future, did everything but. He played with his action figures. He emptied all the markers out of the craft bin and onto the beige carpet. He ran around with a pillowcase over his head. He screamed. After much wrestling, negotiating, and finally, threatening, I managed to get the child into a bathing suit. I packed the car with snacks and toys, located the lake pass, and secured the elder child into the car, but the young one was missing.

I got out of the car, walked into the house and screamed, "Boy's Name, come on!" and walked back out to the car.

After a few moments, the boy ran out, but he was missing shoes.

"Boy's Name, go get some shoes."

He ran back inside, and the older child and I waited. And waited. And waited—far longer than the proper amount of time necessary to retrieve sandals located directly inside the front door. I sighed, turned off the ignition, and ventured back inside to locate the kid.

"Boy's Name?" I said in the foyer. "Boy's Name?" I said in the living room. "Boy's Name?" I said in the hallway. Then I reached the kitchen, and there was the boy, holding a large empty bottle of Tabasco sauce, his face twisted with guilt. The floor, cabinets, counters, and refrigerator were all streaked with red.

"All you had to do was get your sandals," I said.

"But then I saw my car," he said, holding up a micro-machine, as if that explained everything.

"And?"

"And to make the car go, you put hot water in it. But since I didn't have hot water, I tried to put in Tabasco sauce. Because it's hot."

I know what you're thinking; the misconception is cute. In retrospect, it sounds adorable to me too. But, in the moment, standing in the sauce-coated kitchen that I'd now have to clean, after that exhausting morning of trying to wrangle those kids together, I lost it. If this was my child, I may have spanked him. But he wasn't my child, so I couldn't spank him. So I approached him slowly, step by step, and with each step, his face darkened with fear. He didn't know what to expect. How could he? Neither did I.

I extended my trembling hands out toward him, placed them on his head, and did all that I could within the parameters of a non-parent. I squeezed. Yes, I squeezed the child's head. It wasn't a well thought out plan. It was just what I felt in my heart that I needed to do.

His eyes widened between my palms, and I'll never shake from my mind his expression of horror, surprise, and a little bit of confusion. But mostly horror.

Part II

The next summer I was nannying not for two children, but for five. They were beautiful, smart children. A pleasure to be with. Most of the time.

I ran the baths and got them changed into pajamas. I read the stories and tucked them in. Walking downstairs, ready to unwind in front of the television, I found the eight year old out of bed, stacking blocks in the playroom.

"Boy's Name, come on, go back up to bed."

"No."

"Yes, go to bed now."

"No, I'm playing with blocks."

"It's past your bed time. You can play with blocks in the morning."

"No, I'm playing with them now."

"Listen, if you cooperate and go up to bed now without any more fuss, I'll leave your tower here so you can just start back up on it tomorrow morning."

No reply.

"Boy's Name..."

"No. I'm not going to bed."

This is a situation that stumps me. How are you supposed to coerce someone into doing something when they outright refuse? I heard you're supposed to present them with two choices, one of which is obviously preferable to both of you. So that's what I did.

"Okay, you have two choices here: Go up to bed right now without another word, and we'll keep the tower up so you can work on it in the morning. Or, the other choice is I'll knock it down now and you have to go to bed anyway."

No response, other than continual block stacking.

"Boy's Name... I'm going to do it." Nothing. "I really am. Go to bed or I'm going to knock them down." Stack, stack stack. "Okay, last chance here."

Now I was in a pickle. I'd set an ultimatum, and he wasn't listening. But if I didn't follow through, he'd never listen to me again, and that would make for a long summer. So, as unorthodox as it sounds, I had to knock down the child's blocks. So...I did. A little humiliated, I nudged the block tower with my foot, and it crumbled to the floor. The boy looked at me, down at the blocks, and then up toward the ceiling. He parted his lips and wailed.

It is of course at this moment that the parents came home early to find me standing beside their insubordinate son and a pile of blocks.

"Mommy, Alena kicked down my blocks!" he screamed.

And the mother, a very sophisticated and intelligent woman, calmly said, "Oh, I'm sure that's not true."

Because, how could it be true? What kind of babysitter would kick down a kid's blocks? Surely not the one she entrusted to care for her precious little ones. But, seeing my guilty expression, her face fell with disappointment and judgment.

"He wouldn't go to bed," I said with a shrug, as if that justified my juvenile behavior. They couldn't fire me; I was a family friend. So we all looked down at the blocks, heaped as high as the remaining days of summer.

Part III

A family I had never met before hired me to care for their three children over a long weekend. Apparently word of my custodial indiscretions had yet to spread around town.

The house came with two very affectionate

Weimaraners, a sleek breed of hunting dogs. On the first night, while I slept in the guestroom on the ground floor, the dogs went berserk, barking and sliding around on the hardwood floors, growling and snapping.

Of course my first thought was, "Well, there must be murderers outside." I tried to listen over the sound of the dogs' commotion for a window breaking or a door being kicked in. My second thought was, "Maybe the murderers are here for the children and will leave me alone. I better stay put." But the third thought, which followed the second thought quickly enough to prevent me from being despicable to the bone, was, "No, you couldn't live with yourself. You must protect your charges. And if you die tonight, your selfless actions will erase your previous sins, and your story will be retold for generations as the epitome of babysitter martyrdom."

With courage in my heart, I emerged from the bedroom to investigate.

The canines were going nuts, running through every room of the first floor, skittering and yelping. The murderers outside must have been very scary looking.

I poked around and peered into the bushes (through the window—I'm not that brave), but couldn't find anything out of the ordinary. After my search turned up nothing, I realized that, for all I knew, these dogs went ballistic every night at the sight of a raccoon or the moon. I returned to my room and climbed into bed.

"I guess nothing strange is going on here.... unless the murderers were just waiting for me to get back into bed before they strike!"

I didn't sleep a wink.

The next day went smoothly. I was exhausted from the previous night, but the kids largely entertained themselves, so it was fine.

Come dinnertime, Phil stopped by and we started to prepare a wholesome and nutritious meal of frozen fish sticks and French fries. I preheated the oven and pulled the oven drawer open to retrieve a baking sheet.

Inside the oven was something furry.

A curled up animal.

I screamed and ran to the other side of the kitchen. Startled, Phil looked down, spotted the creature, and closed the oven drawer with his foot.

I pointed toward the oven, "What the—"

Phil smiled and calmly said, "Maybe you should settle down so as not to scare the children," and nodded his head in their direction.

I glanced toward the kitchen table. All three kids were staring at me, mouths dropped, eyes wide, horrified.

I took a deep breath, smiled, and sweetly asked, "What was that?"

"A baby possum," Phil said.

"What's a possum?" the eight-year-old girl asked.

"A woodsy animal," I said.

"There's an animal in the oven?" the four-year-old girl asked, excited.

The oven! I lunged for the temperature knob and turned it off before we had cooked possum.

"What should we do?" I asked in singsong.

"Call animal control," Phil said.

I found a phonebook in a drawer, flipped it to the animal control number, and dialed.

When a man answered, I said, "Hi, there's a baby possum in my oven," sure that, being animal control, he would leap into action.

"Yeah, and?" he asked, sounding bored.

"And, there shouldn't be a baby possum in my oven." Maybe this wasn't as obvious as I thought it was.

"So, take it out."

"Me take it out? Isn't that something animal control might take care of?"

"It's still light out and they're nocturnal creatures, so it probably won't wake up. You can take care of it."

I wondered what movie he was watching on his office computer that he didn't want to pause to do his actual job. "I know they're nocturnal, but it's not every day I remove creatures from my oven. How do you expect me to do it?"

"Well, do you have a net?"

"What? A net? I don't know. It's not my house. Can't you just come? I bet *you* have a net."

"Fine. But if it's not your house, I'll need the owner of the house to authorize me to remove the animal."

"Trust me, the owners don't want a baby possum in their oven. I'm 100% sure." But the fact that I even had to say that made me doubt myself. Did they want a possum in their oven? They didn't mention it so I guessed not and continued, "And if they put me in charge of their children and dogs, I think they'd feel comfortable putting me in charge of the animal in their oven drawer."

"There are dogs? Oh, they must be going crazy," he said, sounding pleased.

Luckily, the dogs were outside at the time, but all of the sudden the previous night's outburst made sense.

"When should I expect you?" I asked.

He sighed heavily. "Thirty minutes, I guess."

I hung up the phone and faced the kids with a broad, encouraging smile.

"Can we pet it?" the four year old asked.

"No, but do you want to look up a picture on the Internet so you can see what the animal in the drawer looks like?" I asked.

All three shot up and ran to the computer in the next room. What a fun babysitter I was!

I don't know if you've ever Googled "possum," but it's not a kid-friendly image search. The majority of photos don't look like the snuggly curled up baby possum that slept in the oven drawer. The majority are rabid beasts with bared fangs.

The eight year old screamed, the four year old cried, the ten year old comforted her sobbing sibling, looked up at me, and shook her head in judgment.

Despite his reluctance, the animal control guy

arrived wielding a pole topped with a little net. In answer to his previous question, I'm pretty sure the family did not own one of those. He pulled the drawer open, scooped up our still napping furry friend, and released it outside.

I wasn't sure how to sterilize a baking sheet that an animal used as a bunk bed, so I just ordered pizza.

The next day, to continue the excitement, Phil and I brought the kids to a local aquarium. We saw otters, penguins, sharks, and a whole lot of fish.

Toward the end of the exhibit was a room of taxidermy animals. The eight year old stopped in front of one and said, "Look, it's a possum! Like the one in our oven."

The hulking animal on the wooden stand bore no resemblance to the cute little ball I saw the day before, so I peered over her shoulder to check the placard.

"No, that's an o-possum," I said, emphasis on the O.

As soon as the words left my lips, I knew I was an idiot. For, of course, an opossum could not be an entirely different animal than a possum. They were certainly the same thing. I was wrong and the eight year old was right. Not even the ten year old. The eight year old.

The laughter that burst from Phil was the stuff of purest joy. It was round and bubbly and, in essence, jolly. It made him bend backwards, and then bend forwards. He clutched his stomach. He laughed with his entire body.

"No," he shook his head, "that's not a possum. That's an ooooo-possum," he said. He barely got through the last part of the sentence, so strong was the power of his laugher. And it was contagious, because the eight year old joined in.

There are no perfect children and no perfect parents. But there are certainly hot days and long summers and evenings when the opossum is just going to get in. There will be nights when all a mother wants is a glass of wine and a sitcom, but of course that kid just needs to finish his damn block tower. And there will be times when a mother should keep her head so as not to scare the children, but when her heart will tell her to scream and run to the other side of the room. Mommy is bound, at some point, to say something dumb, and her child will eventually deserve, if not a spanking, then at least a good head squeeze. This is all to be expected. It's a hazard of the job.

That's why I'm not ready, why I'm not leasing a minivan, buying ovulation sticks, tracking my body temperature, knitting baby blankets, taking folic acid supplements, practicing the swaddle wrap on a loaf of bread, shopping in the maternity section, or flipping through nursery paint color samples. It's why when my gynecologist asks, "Should we talk about family planning?" I don't just think, "Hell no, you sick freak," I also think, simply, "No."

It's easy for me to laugh about being an impatient and sometimes ditzy babysitter, but I'm going to have to get a whole lot funnier to find humor in my failings when my relationship to the child is of a more permanent nature. And I'm confident there will be failings; just this morning I ran an empty microwave for two minutes while my cup of coffee sat on the counter, and there weren't any screaming heads tugging at my pant leg. Yup, I'm bound to screw things up. And how do you look a child in his eyes after you've kicked over his block tower like a Pixar bully?

Until I've figured that out, I'll enjoy driving a car without child safety locks and living with a person who, if in need of a head squeeze, at least has a fully developed skull. Or, because I'm not some crazed serial head squeezer, if he spills Tabasco sauce, at least he can clean up the damn mess himself.

Don't Look At Me. I'm Disgusting

Phil went to a conference and left me in the apartment unsupervised for thirty hours. I'd gone so long without being alone that I'd forgotten how disgusting I can be by myself. It took about thirty minutes for my civility to unravel.

The Hunger Games kicked off with a box of Velveeta and a dollop of disregard. If I'm going to brutally honest here, I'll admit that I bought a six box family pack of this Kraft delicacy, just for the occasion.

The cheesy shells meant to serve four heaped golden fluorescent on my plate, which was so heavy it strained my bicep. I carried it right past the kitchen table and into bed, where my laptop waited, radiating the Netflix screen paused on Season 3 of *How I Met Your Mother*. For the next day, I only left the bed for bathroom breaks and to get more food.

I was full after two servings and one episode, so I took an eating break roughly the length of Ted's relationship with Blah Blah. Then I wiped away some cheddar perspiration and returned to the challenge. The artificially colored food was cold and the cheese had dried, but I persevered.

Barney fell in love with Robin, Marshall and Lily fell into a bad investment, and I fell asleep with an almost finished plate of macaroni and cheese resting on my bulging belly.

The next morning looked about the same, except for the addition of sunshine trying to penetrate through the lowered blinds of my shame cave. I swapped out the day-old pasta for a bowl of cereal and tuned back in to see how Ted would deal with his latest heartache.

A bowl of cereal led to toast slathered with peanut butter, which led to pretzels dipped into peanut butter, which culminated in pure spoonfuls of peanut butter. By the end of this session, such a dent had been made in the Skippy container that I had to dive in wrist deep, and my hand emerged smeared with the stuff. I sympathized with Winnie the Pooh and his honey jar. It's a messy business, even for a bear.

My pajamas stained with passing meals—if you can call peanut butter a meal. Bowls, plates, and spoons stacked beside my bed (the kitchen sink was too far to go for the mere purpose of cleanliness). The apartment grew increasingly stuffy, due to doors not having to be opened and passed through. I found a knot in my hair and attributed it to its fierce lack of shampoo but, upon further investigation, discovered the source of its coalescence to be pureed nut, Extra Chunky Skippy Super Chunk Peanut Butter, to be exact. Fuel the fun.

All this, and yet I watched on.

Then Phil texted me that he was on his way home from the airport and shattered my sloth haze. I looked around the apartment. I looked at myself. I saw everything that I had made and, behold, it was not good.

I carried all of the dirty dishes that were piled around my bed to the kitchen and washed, dried, and put them away. The macaroni and cheese pot was still on the stove. It looked like a daffodil threw up in there, and would have to be soaked for approximately a century. As it filled with warm water, I doused it with dish soap, although what it really needed was hydrochloric acid. I mopped up some stray yellow ooze that had globbed on the counter, scanned the kitchen for other dire concerns, and moved on.

The next issue to address was my haggard appearance. Phil doesn't normally come home to a creature that belongs underground but, without immediate action, that day he would have. And, I don't know the laws, but our marriage might have been short enough to qualify for annulment. So, I rubbed the pillow lines from my face and showered, intentionally forcing my eyes up to prevent witnessing the discoloration of my body's runoff water. I changed into a fresh t-shirt and pair of sweatpants (okay, still lazy pants, but at least these were clean), applied deodorant, and ran a brush through my now peanut-butter-free hair. Did I look like a new woman? No, but at least I no longer looked like a homeless woman.

I examined the apartment for other traces of indolence, and found the following: a smudge of melted chocolate on my nightstand from my Reese's Peanut Butter cup binge (oh, did I not mention that part?); enough balled up tin wrappers from the aforementioned binge to play Chinese Checkers; used tissues on the floor of my bedside; a forgotten fork; and a pile of comforter from when it fell off the bed but I was too tired to lean over and pull it back on.

After tying up those loose ends, I took two laps around my apartment while continually depressing the button on an aerosol can of air freshener, spraying its lavender-vanilla scent with the conservatism of an automatic weapon. Then I opened the doors and windows and switched on the fan, reintroducing my apartment to ventilation.

By the time Phil walked in, the only indication of what went on in the apartment without him was the lingering ass imprint on the sheets, the guilty glint in my eyes, and the subtle scent of lavender-vanilla infused self-reproach.

A Tale Of Fire, Thievery, And Mary Higgins Clark

It all began with *That Night*. Not a specific evening in my history, but a book of that title.

The package looked like any other Amazon package. I don't consider myself a superstitious gal, but it arrived on my doorstep on Friday the 13th of April, so maybe I should have known better. I carried it up into my apartment without the slightest inkling that I was the final cog in a masterful criminal plan. (I was probably distracted by the all-consuming desire to stuff my face—a sensation that often accompanies the act of arriving home after a long day away from my kitchen.)

It all felt so normal. When you hear about this kind of thing on the news, you always think, "How could she not know? She must have known." But I didn't. I had no idea. I swear, it looked just like any other package.

That is, until I opened it.

With one smooth slice of the scissors down the center, the illusion bled out.

It was the scent that gave it away. An odor so tangible, so familiar. It smelled like a bike ride followed by two hours curled up in a dark corner with Mary Higgins Clark; a fragrance of childhood afternoons. It stunk of adventure, mystery, and mildew—the aroma of time with a subtle bouquet of knowledge.

It smelled like a library book.

No, that isn't possible. Not even the basest Amazon seller would have the stomach to consign a book stolen from the library, an institution whose only ambition is to introduce the magic of books to citizens big and small, all for the low price of a smile and a few tax dollars. Libraries cradle resources of knowledge, enjoyment, and enlightenment. They are enchanting halls of possibilities, where children can discover the wonders of the deepest ocean or climb the tallest mountain, and where seniors can pilfer toilet paper. Stealing a book from a library would be like slurping up some porridge from Oliver Twist's soup bowl.

Yes, that's what I thought too. I would have sworn that my olfactic sensory cells were deceiving me.

But then I lifted out the book.

The hardcover was wrapped in plastic and secured with tape that had long since lost its stick. A white label on the bottom of the binding read "FIC McD." I fanned a few yellowed pages until I reached confirmation: a red stamp with the words, "Property of Cliffside Park, PUB. LIB." Unnerved, I already knew what I would find inside the back cover but, with a quickening pulse, I just couldn't help myself. I had to face the full, ugly truth, no matter the consequences. I flipped the book and gasped. Not only was there a barcode sticker for faster checkout, there was also an empty envelope for the Date Due card.

But this book would never again need such a card. This book would never again be stamped with a blue or black month abbreviation and date. It would never again be smashed through a Return Book slot. This book was forcefully removed from circulation long before its time, only to be sold on the black market for $4.32. That's the price put on greed by Amazon seller Accessory International LLC, a fitting name for a company that would involuntary make all of their customers into accessories.

Curious about the rightful owner of this book, I decided to do some digging. I googled Cliffside Public

Library. The first headline? "Fire rips through Cliffside Park library."

Books, computers, and town treasures including historical maps and yearbooks were all ruined in the fire two years ago. After extensive renovations, the library was reopened this past September.

But the book I hold in my hands is by no means a bouncing eight-month-old book. This book is riddled with stains and tears. This book has seen kitchen tables, train rides, and the inside of purses. Which means this book is not just the product of a lame money making scheme by a New Jersey Amazon seller. This book narrowly escaped one of the worst fates imaginable. If this book had been returned, this book would have been burned. *That Night* is a survivor that has more than one story to tell, if only you are willing to listen.

Okay, okay. I'll return the book.

On Losing Weight For My Wedding

There's this pair of jeans that have been sitting in my closet for ages. They would be an ordinary pair of jeans, except the zipper begins in the back, traces down the butt crack, snakes between the thighs, until finally fastening up the crotch. These jeans can be unzipped in half, and they're my mom's.

My mother, Faith, wore them in the 70's, when she was a rebellious whippersnapper who skipped her church's night service to go to coffee shops and attended parties that served pot brownies. Only, she didn't realize they were pot brownies. Being a chocolate lover, she ate seven, locked herself in the closet and called my father, telling him "they" were coming and he needed to rescue her. He kept her at his parents' house until she detoxed, and then brought her home.

These jeans are a symbol of her youth. The prime of her life, when everything was a possibility. They represent Before. Before miscarriages or stock market crashes or college tuitions. Before Michael Jackson grew up or Bon Jovi turned country. Before anything wrinkled, bloated or sagged. Before her husband got sick. Before soul patches went out. Before soul patches came back again.

She would build a shrine for these jeans, except that would be sacrilege.

She couldn't throw them out. They were far too important, far too cool, to be garbage. But she couldn't store them in her closet either. That'd be too close.

They'd embarrass her other clothes, her mommy jeans. So, they sat propped on the top shelf in my closet, where they mocked me my entire life.

Like all mothers, my mother often reminisced about the body of her youth, when skin from hip to hip was pulled as tight as a drumhead. She'd stroke the memory, tenderly recalling chicken legs, her tiny waist, and taut arms.

"I was 108 pounds the day I married your father," she'd say.

And I would simmer with jealousy because I was 108 pounds in fifth grade. And I wasn't tall. I didn't know what it was like to have chicken legs, a tiny waist, or taut arms.

In elementary school, I enjoyed sifting through my mother's belongings, the souvenirs of a Faith I'd never know. A Faith without pick-ups or drop-offs or dinner to get on the table. My mother guided the safari through her former self. She handed me the tag that had been attached to a gift from her first love. It read, "To the Beauty, from the Beast. Or is it the other way around?" He sounded like an asshole, and I wondered why my mother dated him for five years, or why she kept that tag for over thirty. But I'd never know, because I'd never meet that Faith. My understanding would only come when I dated my own asshole for far longer than clinical sanity would reason acceptable.

We'd sit in front of her jewelry box and she'd show me the sterling heart necklace her sister gave her on her sixteenth birthday. Or the diamond from her grandmother's engagement ring. Or the lock of hair from when she chopped off her waist-length tresses. We went through this routine, over and over again, memento by memento, and it always ended with the jeans.

I'd sit on my bed while she retrieved them from my closet. She always presented them with the pride of a nationalist waving a flag.

"Now, these, these are retro," she'd say.

And she'd zip and unzip them, telling me that the

zipper used to wedge up her crack, causing the denim to cling to her cheeks like Saran wrap—that's just how every child wants to imagine her mother.

As an eight, nine, ten, and eleven year old, I marveled at the jeans. To wear pants that provocative, that downright womanly, was something I yearned for. But I knew I wasn't ready. It wasn't appropriate. They wouldn't look right, they wouldn't feel right. So I never asked to try them on and my mother never invited me to.

Until one day.

"Here, put them on," she said, extending the jeans as an offering.

By this point, I knew the zipper well. I pulled the slider down the rows of metal teeth, and as they disengaged one by one, from the waist all the way around to the small of the back, the pant legs were almost completely disassociated from one another.

I took off my totally dull pants (tapered acid wash jeans a few years out of fashion, hand-me-downs from my older brother), revealing baggy, cotton, and flowered underwear.

But as soon as I slipped a foot inside the pant leg, I knew the bitter outcome of this experiment, and thus the resentment for the jeans was conceived.

My meaty thigh met great resistance. I didn't have skinny Immordino legs. I had thick, sturdy Dillon legs, topped off with the kind of thighs that rash in the summer from skin rubbing skin too aggressively. The kind of thighs that split jeans at the seam. I knew this, because it happened during recess in fourth grade, and I had to sit with my fat legs pressed together for the rest of the day. (Those jeans were mended that night because, having inherited my thunder thighs from my father, we kept a surplus of patches in stock.)

But, trying on my mother's jeans, I shimmied and stuffed, jiggled and joggled. If I could have sucked in my thighs, I would have. But, since this was not a physical possibility, I hopped. I heaved and hoed. I probably looked like I was performing a tribal dance, or like I was a little bit on fire. Whatever the case, I would not surrender, not after wanting this for so long.

Finally, after much negotiating, and after working up a fine mist of perspiration, both legs were smushed inside.

I bent over and reached my hand between my legs and up toward my back, trying to locate the zipper. When I felt the metal between my fingers, I pulled down.

The zipper pulled up. It had a different goal in mind, and that was respecting a formidable opposing force: my fat ass.

Watching me struggle, my mother smiled, but kept to herself.

I attacked from a different approach. Instead of bending over, I stood straight and looped both arms behind my back. One grabbed the belt of the pants and the other maneuvered the zipper. Without being doubled over, there was some extra give in the rear of the jeans, and the zipper conceded, traveling down my butt crack.

The zipper descended fairly easily. I was able to close the pants up to my inner thighs. It's when I reached down to cajole the zipper for the ascent that it again refused to cooperate.

The V formed by the two divergent metal halves branched out in an obtuse angle. It didn't seem physically possible to bond the teeth together, and yet, I tried.

Holding the slider, I jumped and shook and sucked in my belly. But the zipper wouldn't budge. I flopped onto the bed, hoping my stomach would sink inside itself. No luck; gravity can only do so much. I tried pulling the waist together and then yanking up the zipper. I pleaded with the Lord Almighty. Nada.

I was twelve, and I couldn't fit into the pants of my mother's twenties.

My mother was trembling in hysterics. Finally, she burst into flat out laughter. "I really WAS skinny," she said, as if my not being able to smash myself into her former clothing was the confirmation she'd been searching for.

And though I was disappointed, okay, devastated, there was restitution in the joy of my mother. If she couldn't be satisfied with the body of today's Faith, at least she still found happiness in the memory of yesterday's.

Yesterday's body became tomorrow's when she started Tony Horton's extreme P90X home fitness routine.

I'm getting a little ahead of myself. She began losing weight in Europe.

If touring was a sport in the Olympics, my mother would be a gold medalist. We power walked for thirteen hours a day across Paris. There would be no tourist attraction left behind. At night, I lay down on the hotel bed and felt my heart beating in my feet. She laughed in the faces of guidebooks that read "impossible to see in one day" and had no regard for the fact that my brother and I needed foot transplants.

On our first day in Paris, we walked over ten miles before stopping in a botanical garden. Greg and I disintegrated into an exhaustion-induced nap under a rose bush while my mother continued to pour over her tour book, plotting our next move. That night, Greg and I threatened mutiny, so my mother decided to enlist the Parisian rental bikes for the following day. They were free for the first thirty minutes, so she plotted routes that passed kiosks every half-hour so we could trade vehicles without ever having to spend a euro. God forbid we invest in public transportation.

Speeding on two wheels, the woman thought she owned the streets, sidewalks, and alleys of France. She cut off bicycles, pedestrians, and even buses while Greg and I struggled to keep up, yelling our apologies and delivering friendly greetings to all those that had been knocked over or disserviced by the crazy American bicyclist. "*Mes excuses*. She escaped from *le asylum*. We will return her now. *Merci. Au revoir!*"

Enrolled in Faith Dillon's European boot camp, we each lost ten pounds in two weeks. And that's when my mother caught the workout fever.

My father ordered the P90X DVDs for himself. He bought a pull up bar, a yoga mat, and resistance bands. Little did he know my mother would usurp the cause. When she wasn't cleaning teeth (she's a dental hygienist), she was stationed in front of the television, lunging and lifting at Tony's command.

I joined her for a few workouts. It was embarrassing. My mother lifted twice the weight with double the stamina. Then Tony increased my humiliation by saying things like, "If this is your second workout of the day, you're probably feeling pretty tired by now." And what if it was our first workout of the year, huh Tony? Was it okay to feel tired then? Why can't Tony just get a receding hairline like the rest of middle-aged men?

During the plyometrics DVD, which consists of a lot of jumping, Tony points to a teammate onscreen who's getting serious height and says, "This guy has a prosthetic leg. If he can do this kind of activity, so can you." It was at this point that my mom started jumping higher and I started resenting Tony more than a pair of zip-off jeans.

Suddenly, my mother enjoyed looking in the mirror again. The scale gods smiled down upon her.

She kept me updated on what seemed like her daily weight loss. "Down to 132 today. And there's chocolate cake in the house! Did I tell you my new policy? I eat whatever I want!"

Soon, P90X was too easy for her. I was dry heaving just thinking about inserting one of those hell-camp DVDs, but my mother had to look into other workouts. She started Zumba, and for the first time, learned to dance. She showed us her new moves in the kitchen saying, "Look, I can salsa! Greg, come salsa with me." She began a hip-hop workout DVD and flaunted her "gangster arms" on the beach in Mexico.

One day, sitting together at the kitchen table, we were talking about marriage. She said, "You can't base your choice of partner on looks alone, because looks fade." Then she paused and looked smug before saying, "Except for me. My looks are coming back."

I started thinking about body image and exercise when I tried to lose weight for my wedding.

The bar at which your best weight will be measured for the rest of your life is your wedding day, and that day for me was quickly approaching. I had four months. I got engaged eight months before, and back then had vowed to lose ten pounds before the big day. At the four-month mark, I had gained three.

It's a popular topic. There were just fewer than one MILLION hits on Google for "bride weight loss." And what really knotted my knickers was that Google suggested it when I start typing that search. It wasn't bad enough my Facebook ads begged me to start dieting? Et tu, Google?

It just doesn't have the same ring to tell your daughter, "I was such-and-such pounds on your father and my third anniversary," so I figured I better start cracking down.

Or maybe it does sound better. It was difficult to tell whether my mother took more pride in how thin she was when her scrawny butt could fit into those zip-around jeans, or when she boasted of the weight she was continuing to lose in her fifties.

Until I could decide, I created a list of measures to take that would assist me in my weight loss goal. I supposed I could compose a list of items all beginning with "Stop eating...", but I was trying to be realistic:

> 1) Stop wearing sweatpants every day. The tolerance of the elastic band is fueling the illusion that you can still fit into your less flexible clothing.

2) Try weighing yourself more than biannually.
3) Give sweating a try.
4) Don't spend your workday within arm's length of the refrigerator. In fact, leave the kitchen altogether.
5) Reduced Fat Cheez-Its aren't low fat when you eat the entire box. And nobody buys your claim that it's for the calcium.
6) Eating ice cream every night is overkill. Having seconds is just sad. On that same note, coffee ice cream in the morning ISN'T the same as having a cup of coffee.
7) Remove the Costco tub of peanut butter filled pretzels from your nightstand. Most people don't eat a handful of those on their way to the bathroom at three in the morning.

My mother, my friend Julia, and I went wedding dress shopping. Wedding dresses, like graduation gowns, look good on anyone. Probably because they are both examples of clothing that represent an occasion, a celebration, so they make the wearer look as if she's accomplished something. It's like how everyone looks good holding a trophy. (Shout out here to my 7th grade pal, Abby, for bestowing me with the honor of a Best Friend trophy, a souvenir from her family vacation to Los Angeles—a.k.a. the only trophy I ever got.)

We pointed to dresses in the catalogue and the woman assisting us retrieved them, one by one. The gowns lined up like beautiful soldiers, fashioned by miles of beading, lace, and satin. Each was about as heavy in its own right as the woman about to put them on.

Julia, who was well versed in the art of stage costumes, laced me into a corset, which lifted my breasts to my chin. We ditched the corset, and navigated through the fabric of the wedding dresses until finally zipping or tying me up, with occasional grunts and beads of sweat on my part. Grunting may not sound very regal, but I was inside a wedding gown, so I felt like ogre royalty.

After I was secured inside the vestment, (with bated breath, not because of excitement but for lack of ability to breath), I emerged from the dressing room and climbed onto the pedestal to admire myself in the surround-sound mirrors.

"I think I like the other one better," my mother said.

I exhaled, and with the sound of Velcro being pulled apart, the gown split down the back. But it wasn't Velcro; it was precious, expensive satin. I was the wedding dress Hulk, bursting from the confines of my clothing. I imagined that the sound of fabric ripping in a dress shop was equivalent to shouting *dickhead* during a church service, so I hastened back to the dressing room.

"Hurry, get me out of this thing," I said to Julia.

We continued to discard the dresses by process of elimination, until I was down to two gowns. One made me look like Queen Cool Whip, in the best way possible, and the other like a movie star from the fifties. I had to decide whether I wanted to be a Disney Princess or a celebrity. It was like *Sophie's Choice*.

Finally I went with my instinct. I'm not a Disney Princess. I wear my hair in a bun, trip in high heels, and don't know how to apply eyeliner. It was fun for dress-up, but your gown should be a reflection of you— the essence of your fanciness. And at my core, I'm a movie star.

I'll admit, I had hoped for the chick flick moment. The one in which the girls surrounding the bride-to-be burst into tears, falling at her feet, shouting, "That's the one! You will be the most beautiful bride to ever live!"

But, I brought my mother, who is more of a nodder.

"We can't show the picture of the model wearing the dress to people," my mother said, after I decided on my dress. "It won't do the gown justice. It looks much better on you. You're curvaceous and voluptuous. This model could use a hamburger."

That was the nicest thing my mother had ever said to me. Maybe I didn't have to ditch the daily bowl(s) of ice cream after all.

That afternoon, I showed my father a cell phone picture of me wearing the dress, and I got my tears. That man is always good for a cry.

The Starbucks Stand-off

They say not to bite the hand that feeds you, but that's difficult to remember when the hand is attached to a sniveling little hipster-wannabe Starbucks barista who is withholding your well-earned, richly-deserved Starbucks gold card rewards.

I may not spend enough money to qualify for an American Express gold card. I may not fly enough to have earned miles for a free trip. But when it comes to overpriced java customized to the point the average person is too self-respecting to order, and surely unpracticed enough to actually order properly, I've paid my dues. Sure, most of my orders are a simple tall Pike brew (the cheapest beverage on their menu) but, every fifteen drinks, I get my free beverage postcard in the mail. I step on up to the counter without even trying to conceal the bounce in my step, and request my (deep breath) venti skim pumpkin latte with only two pumps and two extra shots. The name on that drink is Alena, but I'm well aware that they are going to write Elaine or Ulani or, maybe just to be an asshole, Allen. But I'll forgive them, because I just got a $7 drink for free. I'll forgive them because they respected my status as a gold card member, a frequent Starbucks flyer, a constant caffeinater. I'll forgive them because I'm entitled to a free drink, and they know it.

Usually.

But the last time I went to purchase my semi-monthly pound of House Blend Medium Roast beans (which, with a gold card, also comes with a complimentary tall beverage) I (Rodney Dangerfield voice) got no respect. I handed the barista my beans, he asked if I'd like them ground, I said no because I have my own bean grinder, he rang up $11.95 (which is pricey but acceptable if you consider that it comes with a free beverage), I handed him the gold card emblazoned with my name, he rang it through, handed me the beans and.... that was it.

I took an appropriate pause to allow him the chance to inquire about my free beverage order. When he just stared at me stupidly, I said, "For my free tall beverage, I'll have a–"

"If you wanted your free drink with that, you should have told me at the beginning of the order," he said. The hair slicked over his forehead suddenly looked greasier and his dull expression more punchable.

"What? But a pound of beans always comes with a free tall beverage."

"Yes, it does, but you should have told me at the beginning so I could have put it into the register. Now I've already put the order through. It's too late."

As probably could be surmised by now, this wasn't my first pound of beans, and yet I'd never heard this sack of baloney before. I wanted to say, "Listen here you Bieber brat, it comes with a free drink. That's the policy. No qualifiers. It doesn't come with a free drink IF you request it at the beginning or IF you wiggle your ears and wink the order in Morse Code or IF the moon is in just the right phase. It comes with a free drink, period. And if in that puny little brain of yours (yes, the same brain that thought wearing jeans so skinny you had to hop yourself into them made you bohemian) you thought the policy had this idiotic addendum, then why on EARTH did you not, upon seeing my gold card, say, "Would you like the free beverage that you are entitled to with this purchase? If so, please tell me now so that I can punch it into the register." Through those thick-framed Ray Bans, did you think you saw a person who doesn't care for free things? That I would hear such an offer and say, "A free drink? Blech. No thank you. Just the beans, please." Because if that was the case, sir, you underestimated me. I go to real estate open houses for the free cookies. I shop at BJ's at lunchtime to fill up on food samples. I am a woman who seeks out free, not one who'd turn her nose up at a perk she'd rightfully earned.

But instead of saying any of these things, I just stared at him, blinking. A line was forming behind me, but I could neither summon the courage to confront this weasel, nor walk away and leave my tall beverage behind. I was at an impasse—a silent, blinking impasse. And he blinked right back. If Starbucks was a dusty saloon and the Adele track playing over the speaker was *The Lone Ranger* theme, we would have had ourselves a modern day Mexican stand-off—of course with pistols replaced by passive aggression.

Despite my cowardice, Master Hair Mousse was getting my point. He breathed deeply and sighed as long and as hard as his lungs could manage. Together with a dramatic eye roll, he said, "I guess I can make an exception, but only this once," as if retrieving what I was owed was a grave inconvenience rather than exactly the task he was getting paid (with great benefits!) to do.

I ordered a skim latte, and Phil kept an eye on the Purple Pants Punk to ensure that it wasn't a spit latte. Then we hightailed it out of there.

But now we're down to our last bean, and if I'm expected to function tomorrow and the day after that, it's time for a Starbucks run. And I'm telling you right now: if I find Bed Head Fred behind the counter, I'm going to be one cold cowgirl.

*Note: The rewards program at Starbucks has changed since the writing of this essay. And yes, I'm pissed.

The Naked Truth

There are nude beaches fifteen minutes from where I live. This is a fact I wish I knew before setting out for an afternoon in the sun.

Friends were visiting for the day. Up until that point, their previous visits could be filed into the following categories: the time we went to the pitiful winery whose owner was so surprised by our arrival that he said, "Do you realize there are real vineyards only forty minutes from here?" and gave us free cheese nips for our trouble; the time we drove all the way out to the "real vineyards" and I selected the one that held its tasting in a garage; the time we went to a brewery in a garage; and the time we paid sixteen dollars for the Fall Harvest and Seafood Festival, which consisted of joining a crowd of hillbillies of unknown origin to watch crabs race in a kiddie pool.

In an effort to avoid any further debacles, I refused to make any plans beyond the elaborate meals we prepared to compensate for our visitors' risk in venturing from Connecticut, over the Throgs Neck Bridge, and into Long Island.

After we ate, we decided to visit the beach, one of the few perks Long Island has to offer outsiders. We threw around a football and waded into the Atlantic—but these activities alone were far too ordinary for a visit to the island, so the day could not end there.

I'm happy to report that I was not the one who suggested we explore Fire Island's emblematic lighthouse, but I also did nothing to stop it.

Fire Island is vehicle free, so we drove to the parking lot closest to the lighthouse, parked, and walked a mile long trail through beach grass. When we arrived, we climbed it, descended, and then wandered onto Lighthouse Beach, where we immediately spotted a beacon even brighter than the one we'd just scaled: a blatantly naked man.

How often do you stroll around public property and encounter another human being without any clothing? We were startled and confused, but also a little giddy. Intrigued by the novelty of his brazen nakedness, we ventured in for a closer look.

Phil, who just had eye surgery, squinted and said, "He can't be naked. He must be wearing a flesh colored bathing suit. He can't be naked."

But he could, and he was.

I did not play it cool. I don't think I said one coherent word. Beginning from that moment and continuing for the next twenty or so minutes, I was just one long, nervous giggle.

As we moved closer, my unencumbered giggling frightened the nude creature, and he curled up inside of a blanket and hibernated.

At first we were a little disappointed that we scared off this lone animal, when the sighting of one is so rare. But as soon as this one went into hiding, we spotted another in the distance, and this specimen appeared far bolder. He was applying suntan lotion to his lower legs and—OH NO—he was not squatting, but bending over.

We saw one coming straight for us, and the sun glinted off his special area. He was pierced. Oh boy, was he pierced. Right through his Private Eye. We saw one lying casually on a towel among four fully clothed friends. How can you be comfortable lounging in the buff when your pals obviously prefer bathing suits? We saw one sitting naked in the surf, letting the ocean lap at.... himself. I don't know how we didn't notice it sooner, but the nakeds were everywhere. We were surrounded.

"I don't think we're on a regular beach anymore," someone whispered.

Then we saw what appeared to be a mirage: a glimmering man in impeccable physical condition, hands on hips, standing proudly, with no tan lines. He looked as if Michelangelo had carved him from bronze. His presence was palpable. His physicality was deafening. He didn't have to say anything—we knew he was the king of his sandcastle, the sun of this solar system. We felt the gravitational pull, and we didn't like it. It was suddenly clear that if we got too close to him, we'd never be able to leave. We'd get sucked into the mechanism. We'd be caught in the rip tide and pulled out to sea. We'd be no match for this Lighthouse Beach David.

"We have to get out of here right now," Joe said. And we all heard the unspoken end of that sentence: before it's too late.

Our car was still a mile away. We'd wandered too far from the beach grass trail, so we turned on the shore and headed toward what we thought was the exit of this disrobed dimension, toward what we thought was freedom.

As we began our escape, a man wearing nothing but eyeglasses and confidence approached us, casually flipping through a magazine. I'm not sure what the magazine was, but I'm guessing it wasn't a Men's Wearhouse catalog. He stopped and looked us up and down.

"When you're ready, join us," he said, and then continued on his leisurely stroll.

"Thanks," I choked out in the next wave of giggles.

"Oh, we will," Jon said. And that's when the rest of us realized that Jon, our friend of over a decade, a close-talking biologist who looks like a young John Stamos, was disturbingly comfortable in that environment.

We quickened our stride, trying to create as much distance between ourselves and the oiled up Adonis at our backs. We started to relax, started to unclench our butt muscles. My giggles even changed from nervous to relieved. We were in the clear. We could look people in the eye again! But then we saw another naked. And then another. And, suddenly, there were too many to count. Instead of retreating, we had entrenched ourselves further inside the heartland. If these people were of one nude nation, we'd just entered their Tribal Belt—a belt that didn't hold up any pants.

"What should we do? Should I take off my shirt?" Jon asked, a little too eagerly.

"You should take off your shirt," Phil said.

So he took off his shirt.

We passed a bodacious babe shaking a booty so vast her dance threw off the tides. We passed a man wearing a shirt and no pants—a human Donald Duck—standing with his hands on his hips, pelvis thrust forward. We passed a naked drum circle. Yes, a naked drum circle. We passed a man putting on clothes, dress shirt first, buttoning casually, like he had nowhere he needed to be, his Long John Silver swaying in the breeze. We passed a sand sculpture—and even she was naked! We passed a woman with maybe two percent body fat walking, if I recall correctly, in slow motion through the surf. She looked like the African goddess of intimacy; even I stared too long. We passed a naked Jerry Garcia. We passed a nude family who had painted their naked daughters' faces with markings of exotic large cat species. Lions and tigers and bares. Oh my, this was *Eyes Wide Shut* freaky. This was so freaky we considered fleeing via the Atlantic Ocean might be the fastest, safest, most direct way out.

Eventually, we did emerge, but we left a piece of ourselves behind on the beach that day. A naive piece. A trusting piece. A piece that previously had not seen the privates of so many (ugly) strangers.

Joe was shaken by the day's events—so shaken

he probably had to talk himself through getting undressed before his next shower. That night at a local bar, he flinched whenever somebody touched his arm, perhaps suffering from Post-Traumatic Dress Disorder. And he refused to look strangers in the eyes, afraid anyone, everyone, could be a naked in disguise. Jon, on the other hand, spoke with almost a fond nostalgia. "They didn't need clothes," he said. "They were free."

I couldn't believe I was so unprepared, so unaware, when I lived only fifteen minutes away. Although, now that I'm writing this, a vague memory is tickling my brain of a grandmother telling me Fire Island has naked beaches because it used to be a colony for "the gays." But I tend to disregard information dispatched by anybody who plugs an article in front of a sexual preference category. I suppose I should have listened.

Our friends have yet to return to Long Island for another visit. And we? Well, we're still here. And perhaps we were not meant to leave. Perhaps, like the man with the eyeglasses seemed to believe, we were meant to join them.

Section II

What I Think, And Other Insignificant Contributions To Society

I Thought We Agreed To Pee In The Ocean

I thought we as beachgoers had come to a happy understanding on the pee issue, but when my friends and I were wading in the Atlantic Ocean, one of them got out to use the pavilion bathroom.

"Why don't you just go in the ocean?" I asked, indicating to the wide world of water.

Her face scrunched up. "I don't think I can do that," she said, as if it were foul or somehow uncivilized.

"Why not? Hell, I'm peeing right now!" I said, while stretching out my arms into a leisurely sidestroke. And the surrounding swimmers shirked away, because all of a sudden I was the weird one—sort of like when I casually mentioned to some friends that, at night, it's comfortable to lie with your hand down your pants, and they were all, "You mean, like, sexually?" and I said, "No, just because it feels safe, you know?" They didn't.

Anyway, here was my understanding of society's unspoken pact pertaining to urination in various bodies of water:

Pools are definitely a pee-free zone. No ifs, ands, or buts about it. Unless of course the "if" is, *what if I wish to seek revenge on the owner of the pool*; the "and" is, *and on all of the swimmers in the pool*; or the "but" is, *but they peed in my pool first*. Then it's disgusting, and as a society we don't condone such behavior, but that's kind of what you were going for in the first place, so pee if you must, and we hope the owners treated the pool with the chemical that turns pee green and that you are humiliated and exiled from all future block parties.

The other exception for pools is if you are an Olympic swimmer who has earned more gold medals than any other athlete and is worth billions of dollars. In that case, you can admit to peeing in Olympic-sized swimming pools surrounded by fellow but inferior Olympians. Hell, you can admit to peeing on the Olympians themselves, and we will all laugh, because you are the closest thing to a Greek god we'll ever know, yet you are also kind of like a Labrador marking your territory, and that's adorable, you rich Aquaman.

The allowable pee in lakes depends on the circumference, depth, algal density, population of human bathers, and the distance to the nearest toilet. If you can't determine an algorithm to include all of these variables, a personal judgment call will do, as long as you consider dilution potential and the effort that would be required to pee outside of the lake. Just to outline a general principle on the matter, any lakes whose names begin with words like "Great" are probably pretty pee-able, and any lake that your high school friends used to lifeguard at are most likely not. There are no tides or outlets in lakes so, just to be safe, err on the side of holding it in, or go find a tree to squat behind that is far enough from the lake that your pee won't run off into the water along with the next rainfall but not so far that you get poison ivy in all the wrong places.

Oceans, as far as I am concerned, are considered full speed ahead. Open the floodgates. Yellow is mellow. When a body of water has millions of sea creatures the size of school buses floating around and shedding their waste, little old me with my little old pee is the least of your hygienic worries. Plus, I like to stay pretty hydrated and I eat a lot of pretzels, so what's the inherent difference other than temperature, really? Either way, before you know it, a wave comes along and dissipates the concern into oblivion.

(Note: By this logic, you might assume I'm implying a permissible poo, but assuming makes an ass out of you and the sea. I am not suggesting you defecate mid backstroke. I repeat: I. Am. Not. So, please, do not be so moved. The properties of pee oblige it to be so diluted by its generous host that its presence becomes negligible. It nearly ceases to exist. It's almost like it never happened. But the poo? The poo stands alone. The only time you are allowed to poo in the ocean is if you are stranded in the ocean. And I'm talking the *Castaway* no-rescue-boat-in-sight-so-you-might-be-there-a-while kind of stranded. Then it is a forgivable offense, but don't ever speak of it.)

The social pee contract also states that, as a courtesy, we should not alert nearby swimmers to the moment that we are relieving ourselves. Although peeing in the ocean is an acceptable practice, it's still icky to think about, and nobody prefers to be made aware of the urine in their midst. Even I, a citizen who understands the appropriateness of such an ocean release, wrinkle my nose when I hit a suspiciously warm spot, and kick away from it as if an octopus tentacled my legs. What I'm trying to say here is that what swimmers don't know won't hurt them. This is the Ignorance Is Piss addendum.

I respect the I.I.P. code of honor and, when nature calls, I always establish a safe perimeter from my peers. The people I came with are like, "Where are you going?" and I say, convincingly, "Oh, I'm just looking at some ocean stuff over here." But the truth is, I respect most of my friends too much to pee in their vicinity. I was kidding earlier; I wasn't actually peeing as I was talking to my gal pal. I had peed like way more than five minutes before.

So while there certainly are caveats to bear in mind, I was under the impression that peeing in the ocean is a socially bona fide practice. Agonizing over whether or not to just go ahead and do it would be like worrying that your dandruff might flake into the desert.

But I'm beginning to think that I forgot to read the fine print on the yellow memo because, of all my companions at the ocean that day, only my husband backed me on the urination situation, and I've seen him stick his face into a finished bowl of frozen yogurt to lap out the creamy residue, so perhaps I shouldn't use him as my barometer of social propriety. Also, we're the type of people who slow down to inspect the old furniture that people drag to the curb, so I wouldn't claim to be of the highest brow.

Is it possible that there is an age cap for ocean peeing that I've outgrown? Can you be too old to pee in public, even when you are immersed in *17 quadrillion million gallons of salt water? Have I reached an age at which I should (gulp) get out and use the pavilion bathroom?

Also, does posing this many mundane questions in a row make me sound anything like Carrie Bradshaw?

*This approximation was provided by WikiAnswers, so you know it is accurate.

He Can Rotate Our Tires

Phil and I have a crush on our mechanic.

The guy is just so charming. He's the type of person who maintains the perfect amount of eye contact, making you feel important but not scrutinized, and reveals enough details about himself to establish a personal connection without making you wish you never asked the question, "How are you?" He refers to you by your first name even though you've only met three times and the most recent occasion was six months before at your last oil change, so how could he possibly remember? He has a winning smile and sends a personalized thank you note after each tune up, even though the only people to send thank you notes these days are newlyweds and seniors. He has the hardworking, sincere, blue-collar New York accent of Kevin James or Kevin Connolly (never a shortage of Kevins in the Queens/LI area), rather than the spoiled-sounding, nasal New York accent of Marisa Tomei. He goes by the endearing nickname of TJ. And yeah, I guess he's kind of cute, too.

But if there's one person in your life you wish wasn't so charming, it's your mechanic.

The problem with auto repairs is I know nothing about my CRV beyond how to turn it on. And even then, when the key gets stuck in the ignition, I sigh and suppose I have to *walk* to the train station. So when good ol' TJ spouts off buzz words, I nod contemplatively, but we both know he lost me at Honda.

But he's so sweet; he tries to explain it to me. "Imagine you're in your kitchen," he says. "You have a little pot of water boiling on the stove. If you leave it there long enough, the water will evaporate and the bottom of the pot will burn, right? Well, in this case, the water is oil. And the burning pot? That's your engine."

The importance of an oil change is an easy one to grasp. But when it comes to the other parts—the valves and gaskets and spark plugs—I'm quite the dip stick. And instead of asking, "Is it really necessary?" Or, "Can it wait?" Phil and I are asking, "Do you need help moving?" Or, "Would you be our baby's godfather? Sure, there isn't a baby, and even if there was, we have four brothers between us that would be more appropriate candidates than our mechanic, but what do you say, T-dawg?"

Every year I put around $700 into my car, and each time the money is pulled from my bank account I wonder, just for a moment: *Was I swindled? Blinded by the light glinting off his teeth?* But then the thank you card arrives, sometimes with scratch-off lotto tickets enclosed. And I smile and think, "I love scratch-off tickets! That TJ. So thoughtful. Maybe I should stop by his shop to see if he needs a ride to the airport next week. You know, for a mechanic, he sure can afford a lot of vacations."

Driving While Knitting

Have you ever looked into your rear view mirror, seen that the driver behind you is chatting on the phone, and felt tempted to slam on your brakes, just to teach her a lesson? (No? I'm the only maniac? Well, anyway, let's move on.) How are you supposed to feel if you find that the driver behind you is knitting? That's right, this madwoman was cruising down the highway with her ten and two o'clock positions intently focused on two needles working a clump of wool. Her wrists weren't even resting against the wheel.

I assume this was a craft crisis and that she wasn't risking all of our lives just to knit for pleasure. I'd like to give her the benefit of the doubt and believe that this was a matter of national security—maybe Al Qaeda stole all of the President's socks—and more lives would be endangered (how could the President think straight if his feet were chilly??) if she didn't drive while knitting than if she did.

Perhaps an informant in her backseat was bleeding to death and she was fashioning a makeshift tourniquet so he would give her information before he croaked. Or maybe she was on deadline to provide a terrorist with a baby blanket. How can we know what terrorists are demanding for ransom these days? These people are sick—maybe one of them was due at a baby shower and neglected to purchase a gift before the registry ran dry. Those can be desperate times.

Whatever the emergency, I wonder, why not just

ask her passenger to drive so that she could knit without the pesky responsibility of trying not to crash? Yes, she had a passenger of driving age, and it seemed to me that this passenger would have been better suited maneuvering the lanes of Route 27 rather than bearing the sole responsibility of holding the driver's balls of yarn, one in each hand like the scales of balance, a job even the empty seat could have handled with proficiency.

Now, I've tried to knit, and for this activity alone I wished I had an extra set of arms, so I realize that to knit and drive at the same time required much dexterity and concentration. Thank goodness we have people capable of such deftness working for our government. I can't imagine the intensity of their training program, but, if I had to guess, I'd wager it consisted of macramé seminars followed by looming lectures topped off with crocheting workshops. Baby booties camp. I don't know how they found time for lessons of lesser importance, like helicopter piloting and bomb diffusing, but, by god, we must trust that they did.

If the safety of our country depended on me knitting a scarf while driving, I'm afraid we'd all be in grave danger. But not this federal agent. She had it covered, which leads me to conclude that that woman driving behind me was a fine citizen and civil servant deserving of a medal and early retirement. Or, she should be arrested, charged with an indictment entirely of her own making: D.W.K.

The Bathing Suit Blues

Does anybody look good in a one-piece bathing suit?

I can remember a time not too long ago when I thought even a tankini was frumpy, but I've recently taken up swimming as exercise, and bikinis just aren't built for laps. After a few sessions of clutching shifting material to my body while simultaneously trying not to drown, I decided to silence the protesting sixteen-year-old within and spring for the one-piece.

When I took my spanking new Speedo out for its maiden voyage, I was startled by an unpleasant surprise in the locker room: my reflection.

It was positively, absolutely, the most unflattering article of clothing I've ever shimmied myself into. Inside its spandex prison, my curvy figure looked oblong. It made my torso appear stumpier than usual and flattened my ass-ets. I looked like a Saran-wrapped potato.

Staring back at me was not the bikini-donning gal who boldly bears her bronzed skin and unabashed laugh to the free world (ahem, me). Staring back at me was a woman who pays bills; whose jeans used to fit better; who shops at Ann Taylor; who wears sensible shoes; who prefers to be in bed at 9:30 pm on a weekday; who can't have a glass of wine paired with marinara sauce without getting heartburn. Staring back at me was a wife.

All right, I may have accidentally just described

myself. Let's up the ante:

Staring back at me was a woman late on mortgage payments whose kids had been up all night vomiting; a woman who loves her family but only likes them occasionally; a woman who says things like, "Go ahead, cry all you want. Mommy isn't here right now," while locking herself in the bathroom to watch an episode of *The View* on abc.com. Staring back at me was a woman who fantasizes about Clint Eastwood while making love to her husband.

This bathing suit was a cruel time machine to a future I'd rather avoid.

Where, I demanded to know, did I misplace my waist? Did I lose it between the couch cushions amidst the spare change and goldfish cracker crumbs? While I was at it, when did my gluteus muscles de-tone into hunks of cellulite? My backside was crumbling under the pressure of the fluorescent lighting in the women's staff locker room, and those puny S.O.B.'s took the thigh definition with them. For the first time, I confronted a lower half with so many hollows that it seemed to hold hundreds of little faces sucking in their cheeks. I remembered a day when I couldn't grab flesh on my upper leg, and the skin ran as smooth and firm as a tightly drawn tablecloth. Now? Talk about depression.

Alas, it gets worse. I turned my back on this unpleasant time warp of a mirror and shuffled shamefully into the poolroom. A lifeguard—who also happened to be one of Phil's students—greeted me with an enthusiastic, "Hey, Mrs. Dillon!"

And I wanted to push him straight into the deep end because, in those three well-intentioned but sorely-timed words, he confirmed my fear. I was an adult to him—a Mrs. Last Name. To this student, I was a person for whom wearing a one-piece was not only appropriate but also recommended.

If only he knew. If only he knew how youthful I could behave, given the right conditions. Like at my bachelorette party, when I stopped people in Times Square at four in the morning and solicited marriage advice from complete strangers! (One couple made the mistake of answering simultaneously. The woman said, "Spend plenty of time together" and the man said, "Make time for yourself." I think in my unabashed stupor, I said something useful and intermediating like, "Ruh Roh!") So, that's pretty wild, right? That's bikini brazenness right there. And that was just...Oh, two years ago.

Well, I'm sure there's a more recent example of me letting down my low ponytail and really embracing joie de vivre. How about when...Or that time I...

You know what? Who determines what constitutes a more valuable lifestyle? Who defines vivacious living? Sure, bounding around with uninhibited vigor is fun and all, but I'll say one thing: I was so hung-over the morning after my bachelorette party that I spent the entire day in bed. So how is that a wiser investment of this tender age? Am I lame and past my prime just because I enjoy going to bed knowing I'll awaken clearheaded the next morning? And as far as my body goes, my thighs haven't looked this young since I was a newborn baby.

Yeah, okay.

I guess I'll keep the damn swimsuit. What's so great about being a teenager anyway? At least I can rent a car if I wanted. And maybe I'll run for president soon. Who knows? We'll see if I feel like it. And if I do become president, I'm illegalizing bikinis; so enjoy those taut tan tummies while you can, you young beauties. Your days are numbered.

Is This Thing On?

If I could choose one gift off the assembly line of human talents, it would be the ability to sing well.

Scratch that. It would be the ability to eat whatever I want whenever I want as much as I want while never growing beyond a size 6. Hey, if we're dreaming, make it a size 4. But aside from that, it would be the singing thing. If I were a great singer, I would never speak, and people wouldn't want me to. Life would be a song, and I its lead soloist.

Having a mediocre voice does not stop me from trying, although it does limit how much I try in public. Most of my unabashed belting occurs, for the good of humanity, within the confines of my Honda, windows up, radio intentionally cranked to a volume where it almost drowns me out. If I set the volume just right, hints of my voice emerge under the mask of the lead singer and I'm surprised by how good I sound. Anything louder and I can't detect myself at all; anything softer is an unpleasant reminder, and the volume practically turns itself up.

But at the perfect settings, I am Adele. Or Jennifer Hudson. Or Freddie Mercury. I'm the woman you pull up beside at a red light and find mouth agape, head tilted back, her hand shot up as if to say, "Stop, please. This wave of emotion is just too much to bear." But she doesn't stop. She croons until the bridge when her eyes flutter open, and she turns to her right to find you and your passenger laughing and pointing at her.

But if you knew how gut-wrenchingly magical she sounded, you wouldn't think it was so damn funny.

Then The Eagles come on with their tight harmony. And I've gotten a bit too comfortable. The easy melodies of Bruce Springsteen or Journey made me cocky and I think, *Let's crank this up. Let's deepen the emotional complexity.* Alone the melody is catchy, charming. But blended with the harmony it transforms lyrics like, "I gotta know if your sweet love is gonna save me," from playful to urgent. You need the urgency to be soulful.

And I want to be soulful.

So I say, "Okay, Eagles. Let's harmonize."

I hear the stacked thirds of the harmony. I've identified the notes through the first couple rounds of the chorus. So I part my lips, take a deep breath running start, and leap to join in.

Take it eaaasy.

Ouch. That ain't right.

Desperate, I choose another note.

Oof. Wrong again.

I climb the scale.

Yowza.

I outwardly wince, and somewhere a dog is whimpering.

I don't understand it. I hear the note through my speaker and in my head, but what I produce is so far off the mark. All I have to do is match it. I'm not asking myself to do anything a parakeet can't. Yet it's impossible. And although it's just me in the car, I'm embarrassed. My performance embarrassed myself. The volume settings can't help in these cases—it can never be loud enough to cover tone deafness.

I only manage to create harmony if the consonance is such a prominent line, it's practically the melody, like in Journey's "Lights." When it comes out right, or nearly right, I think I'm Josh Groban, and bob my head like a rooster strutting, certain that I missed my calling. I shouldn't be in this CRV. I should be on a stage somewhere.

But god forbid I'm feeling whimsical and I try to create my own harmony line. It's hard enough when I have backup singers to mimic. When I try to develop my own brand of harmony, I sound like the nun choir before Whoopi Goldberg's character intervenes and changes their lives forever. The results cause me to hate myself, and I abandon whatever song inspired me to improvise. I skip the CD until I land on a tune to match my disparaged mood. Alanis Morissette tends to be the best fit. That way, if my vocals sound crude, it only helps the message.

You, you, you, oughta know!

A Love Letter To My Parents' Pool

This was the hottest summer.

I try to suntan on my back deck, but it's like when kids play, *Whose feet can stand on this burning concrete the longest?* Except I have no one to compete with, so I pretty much just walk out onto the deck, am engulfed by raging humidity, walk back into my air conditioned apartment, and...game over. I am the winner, but I am also the loser.

I've been trying to figure out what has changed. Does tolerance for heat reduce with age? Am I in some sort of Long Island ozone oven where temperature is amplified? Have I turned into a vampire? Why am I cowering indoors like a 21st century Emily Dickinson? If I don't go outside soon, the neighborhood children are going to invent scary legends about me, like this generation's Boo Radley. (Can I be Boo Radley and Emily Dickinson, spliced into, perhaps, a Boo Dickinson, or did I just mix literary metaphors? I'll leave that for you to decide.)

Then, it hit me, and it's so obvious. At the risk of sounding like Veruca Salt (Daddy-demanding spoiled girl from *Willy Wonka*—bam, third literary reference. So what if they were all from a 6th grade summer reading list?), I was lucky enough to grow up with a pool and now, for the first time, I am experiencing summer...dry. Well, you know, aside from all the sweat and booze. The lovely thing about having a pool, besides the obvious matter of the pool itself, is that if you are sitting outside and feel moisture trickling down your back, you can convince yourself that it's just residual pool water from your recent dip. On a deck, it's just sweat, and you have to deal with that.

Sun tanning poolside is an entirely different animal, and one that can't be replicated. Trust me, I've tried. And I'm not talking about amateur hour with mini-fans or spray bottles, or the grand innovation: mini-fans with attached spray bottles. I'm talking about unprecedented, avant-garde efforts—like dousing yourself in the shower and then going outside completely wet.

You'd think darting straight from the shower to the deck might be a decent imitation, but, it turns out, it's not. First off, you leave a trail of slick water down the hall, one that you will most likely forget about until you are sliding on it toward the bedroom with slightly less grace than Tom Cruise in *Risky Business*. Second, by the time you race out on the deck and situate yourself with your beach chair and book, you are dry. Pulling a muscle later as you avoid a hallway wipeout will all be for naught.

The other semi-reasonable stab at a pool substitution is lying out beside a stockpot full of cool water. You think—finally, a use for this stainless steel 20-quart stockpot that I requested on my registry but have no practical use for because we are only two people and have no reason to make 20 quarts of anything! But don't celebrate prematurely, for after the ten minutes it takes to fill up the damn thing, you will discover that this measure is also a failure. One, because a stockpot, though too large for only a couple servings of chili, is not the same as a pool, dumbass. And two, now you are overheating *and* you look like a fool on your back deck with views into eight other backyards (two with pools!! Jealousy!!), meaning those eight other families also have a view of you with your feet in a pot, bent over, cupping and dumping water onto your upper thighs and forearms. Now the kids on the block will not call you the neighborhood Scary Lady but the neighborhood Crazy Lady. Happy? Third, now that your sweaty feet have been soaking in expensive cookware, you must boil water in the pot to bring it up to the sterile standards of its intended function—making food. In short, the footbath theory really wasn't worth throwing out your back lugging 20 quarts of water from the kitchen to the deck. 20 quarts is equivalent to 40 pounds, and since you haven't worked out in five months, this process was like asking you to compete in the USA Powerlifting Competition.

There are two expressions that this summer has confirmed to be true:

1) You don't know what you have until it's gone.

2) People with pools have more friends.

If the second one is not a legitimate expression, it should be. I don't see anyone lining up with inner tubes and foam noodles to sit on our deck. But the guy next door? He's either really funny, or people are there for the above-ground swimming hole that takes up his entire lawn. He, by the way, has looked up from his floating lounge chair numerous times to see me on my deck, streaming with perspiration, WITH MY FEET IN A FREAKING STOCKPOT, and has never once invited me over. I would never accept, because swimming in a stranger's pool would be kind of creepy, unless it was really *really* hot out. But it'd still be nice to be asked. I know one neighbor who is not getting Christmas cookies this year. Okay, yeah. Nobody is getting Christmas cookies this year. If I'm baking cookies, I'm eating them myself.

The summer months used to be reserved for getting tan enough that Phil and I could almost pass as an interracial couple. That's all I want in life. Well, that used to be all I wanted in life. Now I just want a pool.

I'm sure there are people down in the heart of Hell (anywhere south of Maryland) that are thinking, "Hey, you spoiled brat. At least you have air conditioning. My armpits haven't been dry since Groundhog Day."

To that, well, I have nothing to say except: Fair point. Why don't you come back when I complain about winter?

What Is The Deal With Knee Hair?

What's the deal with knee hair? Am I right, ladies? And male swimmers who can't spare the drag of a follicle? Or any other kind of man who shaves his legs? I'll take all the support I can get on this little-discussed but extremely pertinent issue. This is an open forum.

It's not like I skip over the knee when shaving, although it always appears that way. I don't jump straight from shin to thigh. The knee hair is just a breed of bristle so evasive, I assume it twists out of the path of the razor Matrix-style, so that when I emerge from the shower, the region looks as if it has never met the edge of a blade.

It's a real mystery because when I'm not running late and actually paying attention in the shower, I address the knee with extra care and committed villainy, "You will not beat me this time," precision. Still, there they remain, mocking me with their virginal softness, having never once been sliced into stubble. Either the hair is indestructible, has ninja agility, or it grows back with Tim Allen as Santa Claus ferocity. I'm not sure which possibility scares me most.

Upon discovering these rogue hairs, I'm always tempted to climb back into the shower—or, on a more frustrating day, go at it with a pair of kitchen shears.

In the dim lighting of my bedroom, I assure myself that they are hardly noticeable. It is only when I arrive at work and swing my legs out of the car that the unforgiving sun spotlights my clumsy work and a certain professor who I may or may not be married to says with a smile, "Missed a spot?"

But I swear, I really didn't. It's just those damn industrial strength knee hairs with Olympic gold medalist dexterity.

What's a girl to do when up against such a force? Wax? But what if we don't hate ourselves? Nair? But what if we want every hair removed, and not just ones selected at random? Electrolysis? See above about not hating ourselves.

Oh, screw it. I'll just wear pants.

My Pre-Cana Questionnaire

When you boil marriage down to its essence, after the passion evaporates, it isn't too much more than a lifelong roommate arrangement. I don't mean to imply that it isn't a big deal. It is. When you say, "I do," you are voluntarily agreeing to board with another person for the remainder of your time on Earth. That's heavy stuff, especially for those who plan on living for a while.

Which is why I believe Pre-Cana questionnaires are useful tools. My dad always said, "Never sign a contract without reading it first," and these quizzes are safety measures to verify that, before signing, you both are in accord. Or, at the very least, are both reading the same document.

The Roman Catholic Pre-Cana course includes a premarital inventory of 156 questions, encompassing topics like finances, sex, lifestyle expectations, and gender roles. I know this because I have sources on the inside. I, unfortunately, never had the opportunity to take this course first-hand because both of the Catholic churches I contacted to inquire about Phil and my marriage ceremony basically told me to go in peace. Apparently they didn't think a wandering former Episcopalian was good enough for one of their precious Italian American sons who has worn a St. Michael's medallion around his neck ever since his Confirmation day. Holy seven sacraments, Batman!

Well, for all of you other wandering former Episcopalians out there who aren't marriage material, you are not alone. And we don't need those exclusive Catholics because I've patched together my own questionnaire of just 24 topics, streamlined down to the bare essentials. How am I qualified to do that? I'm not, but I have a feeling that I have more marriage experience than most Catholic priests.

I don't mean this as a jab at Catholicism. Really, some of my best friends are Catholic. It's just that, having been married for several years myself and having attended an average of four weddings a year for the past three years, I feel that I know a thing or two. Maybe even three things.

Feel free to apply this questionnaire to your own relationship—unless of course you are already married and aren't in the mood for bad news. Then skip to the next essay.

(Author's Note: The below questions are not strictly based off of my own marriage but are also inspired by relationships around me. This is especially true for the very embarrassing items, and I may be convinced to reveal identities upon receipt of a substantial fiscal offer.)

* * * * *

Please answer the following questions with "Yes," "No, but good point. I'll take this into consideration," or "Not applicable because I'm a douche bag who ordered my wife off of the Internet." For the questions that are not "Yes" or "No," don't be a wiseacre; answer accordingly.

1) Do you and your partner watch the same television shows? If not, are they scheduled at different times? If not, are you willing to invest in TiVo?
2) Do either you or your partner enjoy cooking? If the answer is no, are either you or your partner willing to pay the other to perform this service in the currency of

massage or dish cleaning? (This question can be applied to dusting and sweeping as well.)

3) Are you and your partner comfortable sleeping in the same temperature? If not, will the hotter one repress her hatred for the other's heavy artillery of Sherpa blankets that make her sweat blood whenever they are within a mile proximity of her until she explodes into a ball of fire and fury?

4) Do you and your partner both enjoy lying on the beach doing nothing? If one of you does not, can that individual entertain him/herself without nagging me, I mean, the other person, about being bored?

5) Can you and your partner finish a gallon of milk in a week? If the answer is no, will you take the gamble and buy that gallon and end up dumping the excess sour milk week after week, or will you relent and go with the half-gallon?

6) Have you and your partner evaluated the closet space in your future habitation? If there is not enough room for both of your clothes, have you secured a dresser for the man's less important wardrobe?

7) Does your partner know which of your clothes will melt upon application of direct heat, which wool sweater will shrink in the dryer, and which chenille blanket will disintegrate into puffs of poofs if not appropriately laundered?

8) If you are planning on having children, do either of you think it's acceptable to allow a child to run around Starbucks screaming while neighboring consumers are quietly trying to write?

9) Speaking of coffee, do you and your partner both enjoy the same brand of beans? If one of you drinks Dunkin Donuts and the other Starbucks, have you already registered for two coffeemakers to keep on opposite sides of the kitchen?

10) Do you stuff cereal boxes into the nearly full cardboard recycling bin like an ape slamming a quarter into a coin slot, or do you break cereal boxes down and stack them neatly alongside the rest of the recyclables

like a normal homo sapien?

11) If one of you is lactose intolerant but still insists on eating ice cream once in a while, does the other person have a sense of smell?

12) If one of you is an impassioned Democrat and the other a right-winged Republican, have you already canceled the wedding?

13) If you are a dog person, have you asked your partner if he/she likes cats? (The answer may surprise you.)

14) If one of you likes meat on pizza and the other does not, do both of you realize that even doing half-meat makes the entire pie taste like sausage?

15) Is one of you bringing two sword wall hangings from your man-cave apartment? Is the one with good taste cool with letting you keep just this one thing?

16) If one of you is a stingy tipper, has the other perfected the art of leaving extra money on the table when the cheapo goes to the bathroom, especially when you intend on frequenting the same restaurant again and don't prefer spit in your food?

17) If one of you enjoys science while the other is more of a *New York Times* Bestseller type of gal, has the gal mastered her expression of faux interest?

18) Does dirty laundry go ON TOP of the laundry bag, or INSIDE of the laundry bag?

19) True or False: It's okay to staple Christmas lights onto your living room wall. (Hint: Your landlord still has your security deposit.)

20) When you barbecue, does at least one of you refrain from getting drunk enough that you forget to turn off the propane gas?

21) If one of you is far superior at the game Connect Four, is the other one not so competitive that she'll agree to let the game decide every time there is a disagreement? (I believe this question can probably be applied to other games besides Connect Four, but I can't say for sure.)

22) If one of you can polish off a pint of Ben and Jerry's

without pausing for brain freeze, is the other one in charge of scooping the ice cream?

23) Are you both in agreement that washing dishes entails a bit more than simply drizzling soap over the pile and rinsing with water?

24) Oh yeah, and are either of you employed? Do you share the same religious beliefs? Have you discussed family planning? Do you like your in-laws? Blah blah blah...

Eat Before The Clock Strikes Fast!

In an effort to shave off some newlywed pounds (it's a real thing), Phil and I have instated a "no eating after 9 pm rule." Well, Phil treats it as a rule. I view it as more of a guideline.

Ever since the policy has been enforced, there's something about 8:59 pm that makes me ravenous. So I stuff my face with all edible products within reach, my hunger screaming, "Hurry, you're running out of time! When 9:01 pm rolls around, you're going to wish you hadn't wasted these moments debating the damned moral implications!" as if it's Jack Bauer on a deadline. (Okay, when isn't Jack Bauer on a deadline?) I consume like it's not just the last meal of the night but the last meal of my life. And that's how I came to eat a handful of tortilla chip crumbs, grapes, a mouthful of whipped cream, and a spoonful of peanut butter, all within 60 seconds. I don't even remember if I chewed. It's kind of a blur.

This behavior sort of defeats the whole purpose and, though legal, does not respect the spirit of the policy. I get that. I'm not an idiot. I'm just a compulsive binger.

Then, no matter what was gorged leading up to our deadline, I'm STARVING every minute from nine until we go to bed. Maybe not STARVING, but I want to eat. Same thing, right?

I wonder if it's actual hunger talking, or just the glaring fact that I'm not supposed to be eating. Given the amount inhaled a minute before the clock struck nine, science would argue it's the latter.

After this experience, I totally get why Eve ate the apple. It was because she wasn't supposed to. It had nothing to do with the apple itself. I mean, apples are tasty and all, especially if you get a nice crispy Gala in early October, but who just needs to eat an apple? You eat an apple to keep the doctor away. Or because everything else in the fridge is moldy. Or for the same reason you eat celery: it's slathered in peanut butter. Not because you are crazy for apples.

I'll admit that Eve might be more likely than your average person to have hankered a Macoun. She walked around naked and, according to the Genesis illustrations in *A Child's First Bible*, was friends with animals, so it's safe to assume she was a little granola. I'm guessing a juicy sirloin wasn't at the top of her wish list (she was probably more of a tofu kind of gal), and Hostess didn't get their act together until a bit later.

Maybe, standing in the garden surrounded by swiss chard and radishes, sweet produce was as close to junk food as it got. I'll accede to the idea that fruit was Eve's Cheez Its in this scenario. (Although the cocoa bean existed since day three and, if Eve was anything like I am, she was probably enjoying refined chocolate for many moons by the time the orchard was heavy with fruit.) But despite Eve's vegan menu limiting her to treats of fruit, she must have had something more irresistible lying around than a Golden Delicious. I mean, this was Eden. Paradise. When I think of paradise flavors, I think of a tropical blend of mango, papaya, and passion fruit. Come on, *passion* fruit. The sin is right there in the name. So if she were going to splurge, wouldn't it have been on something a little sultrier than a plain old apple?

Let's say she really did just have to have an apple, like some obscure pregnant woman craving. I'd bet there was more than one apple tree in the entire Garden of Eden. How often have you visited an orchard boasting only a single tree? God said he is Alpha and Omega. If I know God, he gave Eve tree varieties with apples from Aceymac to Zestar.

But God told Eve that the one particular apple tree was prohibited. That was the trick. That's why she just had to have it. It wasn't the apple; it was the allure of restriction.

I bet Eve wasn't even in the mood for an apple. If the whole thing wasn't forbidden when that serpent came along and tempted Eve, she probably would have said something like, "Silly snake. Why would I eat a boring old apple when there are kiwi vines just behind my cocoa refinery?"

But the apple was taboo. Off limits. God noticed Eve rounding out on the edges a little and, not wanting Adam whining for a trimmer playmate (a man only has so many ribs, after all), God told Eve she couldn't binge on apples after nine anymore.

So, I get it, Eve. I probably could have summoned the discipline to stave off nighttime snacking if it meant preventing thousands of years of painful childbirth for women everywhere, but you couldn't have known, so I feel for you.

Yes, I am comparing myself to Eve. It may be wrong and grandiose, but I stand by it. I've seen Satan in my kitchen.

The devil is in the Doritos.

Birds That Prey

Not enough people appreciate that birds carry weapons on their faces. Combine those beaks with their ability to fly, and they're an explosive warhead away from being missiles.

If you believe that birds descended from dinosaurs, and if you've seen *Jurassic Park*, you should share my healthy fear of feathered beasts. It's called the transitive property, and you can't argue with math. (To the question, "How many ridiculous statements were just made?" the answer is six. But I have no regrets.)

Given these facts, you can understand my horror at finding two blond girls and an elderly woman at the local state park, feeding a bag full of breadcrumbs to a flock of geese.

Phil and I went to this park for exercise, not an adrenaline rush. If I wanted a brush with death, I would go to Jones Beach on a Saturday in August and yell, "Real men don't wax their eyebrows!" If these females care to act on their suicidal impulses, fine, but do it on their own time—not when it threatens the livelihood of fellow park-goers just looking for a good speed-walk.

So now, instead of the geese floating in the lake at a safe distance like dragons in the dungeon of a castle, they were crowding around their wranglers, squawking and boasting their intimidation, their necks craning like King Cobras about to strike. And yes, I believe dragons and royal snakes are appropriate comparisons.

As I mentioned earlier, I do not have a death wish,

so I clearly could not, would not, walk through this swarm of famished fouls. I abandoned the path to avoid being attacked.

Flash to summer 1995

My family climbed out of the paddleboat, looking forward to exploring the tiny island right off the coast of Watch Hill, Rhode Island. It was not much more than a patch of land peaking out from the ocean, spotted with rough grass and pebbles, but we happily skipped along, probably holding hands and singing the *Brady Bunch* theme song, pausing only to compliment each other.

"Nice over-sized Chicago Bulls t-shirt, Greg."

"Thanks. Cool spandex shorts, Alena. It looks like you're going biking, but you're not. That's sweet."

"Oh, look at this pretty blue rock," my mother said. She bent down, picked it up, examined it, and then dropped it.

Splat.

It was not a rock, but a bird's egg.

Within seconds, the sky turned black. Birds from all over New England were directly overhead. I'm no ornithologist, but I'd wager there were Razorbills, Wilson's Snipes (more like Wilson's Snipers), Bonaparte Gulls (because they are named for a warlord), Fork-Tailed Fly Catchers, Horned Larks, Lapland Longspurs (oops, typo, Long Spears), and Pterodactyls.

These were the original Angry Birds. One by one, they unsheathed their talons and dived and pecked at our heads. I cried, "It wasn't me, it was that lady. Get her!" But the birds didn't care. They wanted blood, and not just of the woman responsible for the splattering of their unborn chick, but of every member of the Dillon family. I don't know what had been in that little blue egg, but it must have been something special, something worth fighting for. Perhaps that was to be their Jesus of Gull-ilee, Prince of Beaks. (Not that I have any assumptions about the spirituality of the feathered. For all I know, birds are Buddhists. But given their penchant for violence, they aren't practicing ones.)

We screamed. We swatted. We ran—over the prickly grass that sliced our feet—to the paddleboat. It was every man for himself; I think I used my little brother's head as a footstep into the vessel. Somehow, we all made it aboard, and my father paddled, literally, for our lives.

I don't like to curse, but that was some Hitchcock shit.

Back to Belmont Lake State Park 2012

As I veered onto the grass, recalling that traumatic day when the Dillon clan was almost struck down by tweeting dive-bombers, a goose lurched, and I shrieked. It turns out that the goose was lurching, not at me but at one of its cohort, to discourage him from a particularly crusty hunk of bread. Greedy bastard. In any case, at my high-pitched squeal, one of the brute-feeding girls looked at me judgmentally, like I was the odd one—as if she didn't look like a kid from a horror movie who would have a goose perching on each shoulder as she said in sing-song, "Come play with me," and stared with deadpan zombie eyes.

It took almost as long for me to stop trembling as for Phil to stop laughing, but I'm not embarrassed by my reaction. Looking at a bird, you can't tell if it has a friendly disposition. It isn't like with dogs where you are greeted with a wagging tail and on-the-back submission that begs, "Please rub my belly!" With birds, all you can see are their beady eyes and dagger-like nose. Who wants to take a chance with that?

Birds are devious by nature. That's why they call a group of crows, not a friendship circle or a nurture of crows, but a muder. Yes, a *murder* of crows. And a pack of ravens? Those are an unkindness. I mean, you can't make this stuff up.

It's no coincidence that Edgar Allan Poe, the Stephen King of the 17th century, chose ravens to symbolize grief and despair in one of his many twisted poems. You'll note that he didn't choose a different creature, like say an otter or a koala bear. That was intentional.

And even the species without such dark resonance are nasty. My fifth grade class hatched chicks in an incubator, and I convinced my mother to adopt two of them. I had romantic images of skipping around our backyard, dipping a hand into my apron pocket and tossing feed at them while they chirped a song about my beauty and humanity. Well, they were cute at first, but these chicks grew into roosters who were so aggressive and smelly that my entire family was too afraid to go into the backyard that summer. We watched longingly from our kitchen window as they strutted around the swimming pool, staking out the territory without any intention of enjoying the water. They even attacked our family Irish Setter until she gave up her dog bed. Cocks.

Think about it—has a bird ever been portrayed as lovable and heroic in the media? Don't be fooled by the long lashes and chirpy voice of Tweety Bird. What is he other than a cross-dressing, conniving canary who lives to frame his foe (this may be the only time I sympathize with a cat). Then there's Iago, the cunning macaw who roosts on the malice of Jafar. "But what about Mother Goose?" you say. Please, I've seen geese. That hag would drown her biddies for a good piece of Italian bread. And what do we really know about Big Bird? Where did he come from, how did he get so big, and what does he do that he can afford to nest in a brownstone right off Sesame Street?

No, birds cannot be trusted, and if Phil makes good on his threat to surprise me at home with a taxidermy raven, I'll add husbands to that list.

Lotzah Matzah

On April 15th of this year, Passover ended and Jewish people nationwide tossed their remaining matzah to the side and sank their teeth into the doughiest, yeastiest, breadiest bread they could find. Actually, I'm not positive that this is true. It's an educated guess based on the fact that on April 15th, grocery stores started handing out boxes of the unleavened cracker for free, and since grocery stores aren't normally in the habit of giving away food (as this would be a poor business model), I can only assume that after a week of the stuff, our Jewish brethren weren't begging for an encore.

Phil and I took four boxes. We are big fans of free, especially of the food variety. But upon the first bite, we understood why this was no-charge fodder.

It isn't bad, necessarily. In fact, it doesn't taste like much of anything. If I had to identify the notes of flavor in matzah like a wine connoisseur would at a cabernet tasting, I'd say, "I detect hints of toasted cardboard with subtle suggestions of other tasteless provisions that you eat strictly for nourishment, like say... flour and water." Which makes sense when you read the ingredients on the label. "Flour and water only." Only. How often do chefs underscore how little there is in their cuisine?

I'm sure the makers of Aviv Passover Matzos include the word "only" to confirm for those observing

Passover that their meal is as bland as it should be. But for a gentile like me, the "only" is not just a little hilarious but also completely unnecessary. I could have told you that it was flour and water only when a bite of the stuff made my mouth so dry that I expected dust to escape through my lips in a puff cloud.

Needless to say, Phil and I haven't been sneaking late night snacks of the sacred delicacy. This chow isn't designed to be a treat. I get that now. It's designed to make the consumer consciously aware of the resoundingly mediocre experience that chewing it entails. And, since that is the intent, matzah, you are a wild success. But, since I am not a Child of Israel, since my ancestors did not suffer at the hands of Egyptians until finally being liberated by their gracious God and the mostly obedient Moses, there is little reason for me to commemorate The Tenth Plague, in which God killed all of the Egyptian first-borns in His ultimate warning to the civilization, but *passed over* the houses of his chosen people. I certainly respect the Festival of Unleavened Bread, but I'm mostly Italian and prefer my bread as leavened as possible; it's easier to wipe up residual tomato sauce that way. The other half of my heritage is Irish, and they had their own set of problems. I'd be happy to honor their famine by consuming all varieties of potatoes for eight days. No offense to matzah, but potatoes are just a superior carbohydrate, unless of course there is some way to mash or fry matzah that I'm not aware of.

Four months later, Phil and I are down from four boxes to three and a half boxes, and we've been mindful of its presence. It isn't tucked away in the back of the cabinet. It enjoys prime real estate on top of the refrigerator, next to cereal that we eat on a daily basis. We've been consciously struggling to consume the matzah. I even looked up recipes and got really excited when the first result was an article entitled "100 Recipes for Matzah." But it turned out that the author was being a bit generous with the word "recipe." The article really should have been called "100 Things to Schmear on Matzah." I have to admit that I was a little disappointed. After 5,000 years of annual matzah leftovers, I expected a more innovative use for it than "as a cracker."

At this rate, we'll never get through our supply by the next post-Passover giveaway. And, again, we just can't resist free. So unless I'm willing to double my supply, and this really isn't an option since I've flat out run out of storage space, I better accelerate the expenditure. To speed things up, I've constructed a list of alternate uses for matzah:

• Placemat

• Karate chopping sheet for a child's belt test

• A customized graduation cap topper

• Frisbee

• Mulch

• Framed as abstract religious art

• Bookmark

• Building material for the fourth pig

• Ninja training: line up a row of matzah sheets for ninja apprentices to run across. If the matzah shatters, they are not yet ready.

• Break into tiny pieces and toss at just-married Jewish couples in lieu of rice

• Hand fan

• Take on a hike and leave behind as a crumb trail. You don't have to worry about the birds eating it. They won't. Leaves and twigs have more zest.

- Regrind it back into flour

- If you are a secret agent, you can leave it outside your hotel door. When you hear the matzah crack, you'll know the villains are about to Uzi their way into your presidential suite, so you should hide inside the tuxedo hanging in your closet.

- Parchment

- Rosh Hashanah party confetti

- Hang as a baby mobile (and this would use multiple sheets! I'm going to be a hit at the next family baby shower!)

Or, I suppose, we could just eat it. Despite my complaints about the "100 Recipe" piece, the woman had a point: matzah was made for slathering—well, not literally—and is also tasty when soaked in something yummy, like soups or chili. It's a modest fare, but the nice thing about that quality is it doesn't distract from the taste of whatever you decide to spread on top of it. It serves as a silent vehicle for flavor, and makes me look a whole lot classier than when I just spoon Nutella directly into my pie hole.

The In-Flight Entertainer

It is somebody's job to screen and select movies to be featured on flights, and I wonder why it is not this person's top priority—nay, ONLY priority—to veto movies whose plots include an airplane crash.

Maybe this is just me, but when I'm caught in a metal tube that's careening through the sky at 500 miles per hour at an altitude of 30,000 feet, pretty much the last scene I want to watch is of a character in my situation where, instead of landing safely, something goes horribly wrong: the plane drops, the wings tear off, passengers are sucked into the atmosphere, other passengers hit the ceiling, and general chaos ensues while the pilot loses control and the plane nosedives. Perhaps I'm a wimp, but when I look around to find myself in a scene with the same disastrous potential, I find these images unsettling. Show me war; show me horror; show me tragedy—just so long as the war is not with fighter jets, the horror is not engines failing, and the tragedy is not an unsuccessful emergency landing.

The particular movie I selected to view on my flight last year was not centered on a crash, but the depiction was graphic and realistic. When the scene began, I was confident a movie with such content would not be available on a flight and expected the scene to end peaceably. Some heroic passenger (most likely the masculine leading man) would kick down the cockpit door, seize the controls, and guide the plane and its passengers to safety, thus inspiring the viewer with renewed faith in humanity and trust in the guy sitting next to her. But, when all of this failed to happen, and the fictional plane actually crashed, I sat, blinking. My pulse quickened. Where were those emergency exits? Were the passengers in the emergency exit row strong enough to get the damn things open? Could I trample them on my way to safety? I waited for the oxygen masks to drop.

I'll give this much to the movie screener: the film did not focus on the catastrophe of the plane crash. No, the crash was only the inciting incident. I thought, well, okay, if they approved this movie even with the plane crash, surely the remainder of the film will compensate for that trauma. Yes, people died, but the surviving passengers must triumph over tragedy.

Wrong again.

The crash resulted in a slaughterhouse of dead bodies, the blood of which attracted a pack of ravenous and conspiring super-wolves. The survivors of the crash spent the remaining sixty minutes of the movie attempting to outwit these devil monsters. Not one character succeeded. They all suffered in arctic conditions for several days, watching one another be attacked, before they themselves met their ghastly end at the sharp points of fangs and claws.

The moral of the story, in simple terms, was: if you ever find yourself in a predicament involving a plane crash, do yourself a favor and die in the accident.

You would think that whosever job it was to handpick the movies available for viewing would have considered the emotions such a "moral of the story" might evoke in the 400 passengers trapped in Flight EI0109, all of whom now had no way of combating such a destiny. You would think that the movie screener would have passed on this film in Act I, as soon as the plane began to rattle, and certainly would have stamped her veto when she discovered that not one character in the film came out alive.

I imagined the movie screener at work, sitting in a

space designed to look like an airplane, complete with overhead compartments, whirring white noise, a flip-down tray table, and access to a toilet that sounded forceful enough to take her in its flush and drop her somewhere over a large body of water.

She greeted her colleagues wearing sweatpants, a messy bun, and carrying an eight-dollar neck pillow. Then she walked into her pressurized cubicle, buckled herself in, stowed her purse, released her office chair from its upright position, and began to enjoy the in-flight entertainment.

Every hour or so, a begrudging coworker plastered on a uniform and a smile and visited the movie viewer's cubicle. On one visit the coworker served up a mini bag containing approximately four pretzels; on another he/she poured water from a liter-sized bottle into a little plastic cup designed to hold only a few meager sips; and on a final visit, the coworker arrived with a plastic bag to collect the trash—or, if the flight experience was simulated to be over the UK, the rubbish.

The movie screener saw this movie and made a grave mistake. But hey, we all make mistakes on the job. Maybe before calamity struck, she took a bathroom break and was sucked down the drain.

Unless...

Unless this cinematic choice was intentional—some twisted "how to"—a subliminal extension of the pre-takeoff safety demonstration:

In the event of an emergency, please assume the bracing position. If we land in water, a life vest is located in a pouch underneath your seat. If we land in the Alaskan wilderness, and you have the misfortune of living through the impact, poison is located between the armrests. Trust us, you're better off.

What a sicko.

A Rant By Alena Dillon, Starbucks Gold Card Member

I am sitting in Starbucks, writing. Starbucks is my office, my nine to five. I used to work at home on my kitchen table, but after four days of repeating a typing, eating, peeing cycle until Phil got home, I realized two things: One, I hadn't left the house in four days. Two, this recluse lifestyle was allowing me to develop some socially unacceptable habits. I used to be a person who DIDN'T sit with a spoonful of peanut butter and a hand down her pants.

Phil and I moved to Long Island for his job. Growing up in Connecticut with extended family in Long Island and New Jersey, I was bred to resent them both. I'd like to say we really only hated the George Washington and Throgs Neck bridges, the hormonal gatekeepers of Wrong Island and Screw Jersey that don't let you pass without paying overpriced tolls and sitting in bumper-to-bumper traffic that would have made Lewis and Clark think, *Crap, I should have stayed home.* But the truth is, the GW and Throgs Neck bridges are so poke-your-eye-to-distract-yourself painful that they begrime their respective destinations with slimy, sitting-in-the-car-for-too-long film.

Phil and I dread going "off-island." We've tried everything to assuage the commute. We travel at strategic hours, when we assume nobody will be on the road: one in the morning on a Tuesday, midnight on

New Year's Eve, or smack dab in the middle of the Super Bowl. But then there is roadwork or lane closures or a freak accident with a motorcycle and a seagull. Any way we slice it, we are doomed.

Then we try accepting the inevitability of traffic: burning CDs with our favorite songs, packing snacks and beverages, and really embracing the road trip adventure mentality. But the CDs skip, the snacks make me carsick, and we have to pull over in the heart of the Bronx to find a McDonald's bathroom because the Super Slurper iced coffee makes me have to pee like a racehorse.

We can't win. I don't know what all the fuss is about, but everyone fights to get into Long Island and New Jersey, and the highway is a parking lot. Travel sucks, and it's best just to acknowledge that the trip will be three hours of misery that we'll never get back. That way, we won't be disappointed.

Over the years, I have associated family members with the demands required to visit them. My aunt sounds like a car horn. My uncle looks like a tollbooth. My cousin moves in stop and go. Now that I live in Long Island, I'm afraid that's what I look and sound like to my peers, and the thought makes me shiver.

So far, I've only made two friends in Long Island. The first was Rosa Bianco, the slightly sweaty instructor of our Italian cooking class who, when I asked if sausage bread could be made with turkey sausage, stilled her hairy arm over the garlic she was mincing, looked at me and asked, "Why you wanna ruin it?"

The second connection made was with Donny at Dough Boys Pizzeria, who gave me free garlic knots with my broccoli pie, and if that isn't friendship, I don't know what is.

Well, Donny is sending me mixed signals. First he gives me free delicious dough. Then, last week, I walked into Dough Boys to pick up my weekly pie, about to slug good old' Free Knots Donny in the shoulder, when he asked me, "So, how'd you hear about us?" And just like that, I lost 50% of my friends. Apparently the last year of being my pizza parlor and number five on my speed dial meant nothing to him. I wonder if he saw the pain on my face. I wonder if he thinks playing with a girl's heart is some kind of joke, or if he just underestimates the message sent by complimentary Italian food.

Back to Starbucks. I'm a gold card member, meaning I have a shiny gold Starbucks card embossed with my name, which I recharge when my coffee funds get low. When my barista chirps, "$1.56," and I hand her my card for payment, I'm not sure whether to be proud or embarrassed by this gaudy mark of café status. Phil would say I'm alarmingly self-righteous about it.

One afternoon, he was sifting through a pile of mail on the kitchen table while I flipped through a month old *New Yorker* on the couch. (They come every other week and are mostly about politics. How's this girl to keep up?) I'd already glanced at the mail, and every letter featured our name and address through a plastic window on the envelope, so I knew it was all boring. AKA, a job for Phil.

I was deciding if I actually understood a political satire piece or if I should just pretend that I did when Phil said, "Oh look, I'm qualified for a gold card."

My stomach dropped. You don't just qualify for a gold card willy-nilly. It takes work. Commitment. You must frequent Starbucks and exercise patience. I had to register for a card, enjoy thirty coffees, and then wait four weeks while my prize took its time to arrive, a period that required great restraint—restraint that was a challenge considering all the caffeine I'd ingested. I had tweaked while opening the mailbox and, when I discovered all bills and no glowing gold card, it took all I had not to punt the nearby garbage can.

I knew for a fact that Phil had only enjoyed four or five beverages, tops. And that amateur received a gold card without breaking a sweat? This was an outrage.

"Hey, you haven't earned it!" I said, with tangible

bite.

Phil turned to look at me, slowly, as if facing a rabid dog, and held up the envelope in his hand to reveal the logo for American Express.

"A gold credit card, not a Starbucks card," he said.

He wasn't a threat after all. I nodded approval, and when he thought I wasn't looking, he mouthed, "Wow."

Back to Starbucks. Again. Every day I burrow in an overstuffed chair in the corner of Patchogue's Starbucks, my laptop plugged into an outlet and a tall pike brew on the table to my left, writing. Writing in this establishment to stay caffeinated and sufficiently surrounded by people, thus preventing regular nose-picking or belching—to keep me properly civilized.

Not that Starbucks hosts the most refined citizens. More than once I've been stranded on the john because the user before me failed to report an empty toilet paper roll to the appropriate personnel. With Starbucks's open bathroom door policy and wildly accessible wireless network, it's no wonder that such delinquents run rampant.

That's right; Starbucks now has free wireless Internet for all. It used to be reserved for gold card members, but now any shmoe can check his mail. Doesn't bother me, except being a gold card member used to mean something. Anyway, I'm glad I can access my Yahoo. Glad I can press the refresh button every ten seconds when it doesn't seem like a word in the world could make the sentence I'm writing coherent. Glad I can receive what feels like my weekly rejection letter, just when I finally get my juices going again.

But that's the life of a writer, specifically one who only gets an unpaid publication every other year. My mother wanted me to be a pharmacist. A superintendent. A speech pathologist. A dentist. When I went for an English degree, she rooted for library science. When I went for my MFA, she got desperate.

"Electrician? Mechanic?" She had many dreams for me, and none of them were to be a writer. But I don't blame her. If a parent's dream for their child was that they'd become a writer, I'd wonder if maybe that child would be safer in someone else's care.

"Well if you're going to write, can't you at least write fiction? Have you no imagination?" my mother said. "Reading your work, it's like hearing the same joke twice." That's when what I'm writing is funny. When it's personal, she says, "Have you no shame? No shame at all?" And this is true; I have no imagination and no shame. But I do have free refills. After all, I'm a gold card member.

My Eulogies for the Living
Or, Author of the Book of Morbid

I compose eulogies while I drive.

I don't enjoy doing it. I don't find it fun. It's completely involuntary. I'll be cruising down the highway or zipping around residential streets on my way to the grocery store, and my mind will wander from a friend's upcoming birthday to zodiac signs to cancer until my husband or father or brother has cancer and, oops, now he's dead. Before I know it, I'm dressed in black and standing at a pulpit, describing how he affected my life. He was filled with goodness or integrity or laughter. He saw the best in humanity or sacrificed or enjoyed life. The world was a brighter place with him in it. (I do this to the females in my life also. The use of "he" was just for the ease of pronouns.)

Back in the real world, where my loved ones are alive and basically well, I arrive at my destination with eyes red and puffy from tears. Sometimes, if my brain really commits to the speech, I won't even make it to Stop and Shop. I'll be pulled over in Shell gas station, sobbing. It's a real problem.

Studies show that the intent of dreams is to test your body's reaction to certain situations, and I think that goes for daydreams and day-mares as well. Like pretty much everybody but sociopaths, my biggest fear is losing family and friends. So perhaps my mind's compulsion to create dark skits on the road is a subconscious defense mechanism so that I'm not caught completely off-guard if tragedy does strike.

Or, more likely, I'm just demented.

The twisted tendency extends beyond the walls of my Honda CRV. It's pretty much wherever there is quiet and my imagination has more than three minutes to roam free. It's happened in my office, at church, and in my apartment. There have been multiple occasions when, lying in bed, Phil hears me sniffling and he groans, "Are you writing my eulogy again?"

Sadly, the answer more often than not is, "Yes, yes I am. And it's beautiful."

To be even more honest, though, and this is embarrassing, the madness doesn't end there. I've written eulogies for myself, too. This has only happened once or twice, and the sadness I feed on in this scenario is not my own, but the pain of imagining my loved ones in bereavement. As I'm writing this, I hear how egotistical it sounds, like, *Man, if I were dead, my family would be saaaaad.* But, damn it, it's true! They would be. At least they better be. And if there is a fear second in size to losing my family or friends, it's causing them pain. So, there, I'm not arrogant. I'm practically a saint.

A few nights ago I was having trouble sleeping and, wham, bam, boom, I'm dead.

Phil is dressed in a black suit, standing at the pulpit of my childhood church, addressing a sizeable crowd (this is my nightmare, I can have the President in attendance if I'd like). He's trying to be strong; he wants to get through this but, my god, what an aching loss. He takes a deep breath and speaks from the heart. It's absolutely breathtaking. Who knew a math professor could come up with such poetry? It's almost as if his deceased wife, an extremely talented writer, composed it for him before she died. But that couldn't possibly be.

"Phil," I said in a whisper. His back was to me, so I poked him, testing to see if he was still awake. He shuddered. He snored. He was asleep.

Well, I didn't want to disturb him, but what if I fell

asleep and forgot this little glint of brilliance in the morning? Could I forgive myself knowing that Phil would never have the opportunity to share such a gem at my funeral? (He had already agreed to die after me so I'd never have to mourn him. Thus, his presence at my funeral is kind of a given.)

"Phil," I said, more urgently. He stirred but didn't awaken.

"Phil!"

"What?" he asked, annoyed. He can be sensitive.

"Oh, good, you're awake. Listen, I came up with something for you to say during my eulogy, but I'm afraid I'll forget it. So you have to remember."

"This ought to be good," he said, turning onto his back.

I breathed in through my nose, calming myself so I could articulate this line with the utmost grace. This is the remembrance he would utter at my funeral. The first time he heard it should be a tranquil experience.

"Okay, this is what you'll say about me." I delivered the following words with care and love, "She was the pilot of our lives. I just sat beside her and watched her fly."

Phil stared at me for a moment—I assumed digesting the magnificence. Then his face broke. Not in tears, but in laughter. Crippling laughter. Laughter that was wildly inappropriate after hearing your wife's eulogy at two in the morning.

The harder he laughed, the more my mind focused out of its middle-of-the-night haze, and I heard my tribute as if for the first time. It was like watching your second grade talent show performance ten years later. I cringed.

Aside from the stilted metaphor, the self-aggrandizing was almost too much to bear. It sounded as if Phil was just a passenger at the mercy of my control. This sentiment is so obvious in the phrase that I'm embarrassed to admit, when composing, it wasn't my intention. I don't know what my intention was—it was two in the morning—but I'm pretty sure I didn't want my post-mortem self to come across as some maniac aviator who took Phil hostage. What in the privacy of my own contemplation sounded lyrical, out loud sounded more like the product of a hack songwriter who tried, but could never live up to, his idol, Stevie Wonder.

Well, Phil is a good man, but not so good that he was about to turn over and go back to sleep, letting this gaffe go. After his hysteria subsided, he wiped the joy tears from his eyes and turned to me, looking serious.

"Alena, I just want to tell you something," he said, really fixing me in his stare. "You are the cabdriver of my life. And you really shouldn't take 5th at this time of night."

Tick Tock Goes My Beauty Clock

My beauty has an expiration date. Or, more accurately, it was slapped with an expiration date. While eating an unusual interpretation of Caribbean jerk chicken in a university cafeteria, a hex was put on my face.

A young Latino gentleman* of a culture that prizes female allure above health and happiness was possessed by a mid-chew vision. His eyes rolled to the back of his head, his jaw fell slack, and a voice I can only identify as Satan poured forth.

"Alena, you're pretty now, but you've got some deep smile lines, and in five years..." He came back into consciousness just to twist his face in disgust, as if somebody pulled back a bandage to reveal the grotesque stitches of my future. After he expressed his revulsion, he reverted back into the passiveness of possession and droned, "You better buy some anti-wrinkle lotion or something."

He then shook off the clairvoyance, as if it were nothing but a fly landing on his arm. Then he resumed eating, casually, evidencing no awareness of what had just transpired.

Now I was staring at two Caribbean jerk chickens.

We were both members of the Capoeira club, a Brazilian martial arts group taught by a "mestre" who, when I first started, convinced me that Brazilians greet one another with kisses on the mouth. I was eighteen when I first joined, actively open-minded and naïve bordering on stupid. So as my group traveled to different Capoeira events across the northeast, I made it a point to greet all Brazilians with a kiss on the lips, thinking I was worldly and culturally sensitive, when really I was just the girl who kissed everybody on the lips.

At that moment in the cafeteria, I'd been in the club for three years. In fact, I was the president. The all-powerful, wise, strictly hug-only, presidente. And across from me sat one of my minions, who dared to divine the imminent demise of my attractiveness.

I can't imagine that I looked so beautiful to begin with. We'd just come from training, and I am not a delicate exerciser. Some girls in the club wore fashionably v-cut sports bras and weaved their hair into a strong but sexy Lara Croft braid. Not me. I wore baggy clothes and knotted my tresses into a bun at the top of my head. As soon as my heart rate climbed above 100, the hair at my temples instantly poofed and my face radiated a rash-like red that required multiple hours to recede. Plus, I smelled.

But appearances didn't matter. We were martial artists. We kicked and we dodged and we struck. Right?

Wrong.

This Latino gentleman, this peasant in my court, was warning me that the days of my appealing physicality were limited. And, looking at him, the smile disappeared from my face. But its lines, apparently, did not.

The other diners and members of the club just blinked, unsure what to say. Finally, Phil, who is now my husband but at the time was a friend and fellow Capoeirista, broke the awkward silence and said, "Man, Latino gentleman. You're a real asshole."

"What?" the gentleman said, hands up, looking genuinely surprised. "I'm being nice. Better she knows now while she's still got time."

Have I mentioned that he had the jowls of a basset hound?

I can't say for sure what he was implying by "while she's still got time," other than that he didn't "got" a handle on proper English grammar. Did he mean while I still had time to delay my disintegration with facial muscle stimulation? While I still had time to enjoy the perks of having feminine wiles: a last free drink, a last held door, and a last coat draped over a puddle? Or perhaps, while I still had time to secure a husband? You know, before it was too late.

It was at this point that I should have dove across the table and grabbed him by the too-tight collar. "Do you know what the average woman goes through before presenting herself to the world? Have you seen how teeny tiny Spanx are before we stretch and squeeze and stuff our bodies into them—god forbid it's a hot day and we're a little sweaty? Well, believe me, the Spanx race should be added to one of those Japanese game shows. And have you ever been plucked or waxed? You know what, don't bother answering. The shrubbery between your eyebrows went ahead and answered for you. Well, imagine ten band-aids all over your crotch. Yeah, it's a special circle of Hell reserved for women and male Speedo models (god bless them). Then there are nail products and hair products and the products for the products. And of course, makeup. Sure, I may not use any of these myself, but from what I hear, a little foundation on that blemished chin of yours would go a long way. And yet you have the audacity to say that I have five more years before I'm more lined than a city street map—you must think you're some Enrique Iglesias wrapped gift to women. Sorry to break it to you, but, as far as male singers go, you're really more of a Meatloaf."

Instead of giving him the verbal beating he deserved, I simply said, "Thanks, Latino gentleman. That's quite the public service announcement." I saved my retribution for the next Capoeira class. You know what they say: Revenge is a dish best served as foot to your enemy's ham shank of a head.

After dinner, Phil caught up with me, touched my arm, and said, "Latino gentleman's an idiot. Don't listen to him."

I rolled my eyes and flashed my best, albeit, lined smile. "Don't worry. I won't."

What did the Latino gentleman know, anyway? How could he diagnose my shelf life, as if he were some wrinkle soothsayer? Five years—so specific. What did he expect to happen at the close of that fifth year? Would I one day look like my youthful self, and the next like the old hag queen from Snow White, the one with the poison apple? Or was my face going to experience a steady withering, like a dehydrated rose? In any case, there isn't anything wrong with a couple of lines. Who needs botox? You know what I could fill those smile lines with? Funny memories.

But I'd be lying if I said I didn't take an extra pause in the mirror that night. And there they were. I saw for the first time that, even when I looked serious, ghosts of smiles past left their mark around my mouth, like faint, spirit parentheses. I puffed out my cheeks to stretch the lines, but they remained. And when I went grocery shopping the next day, Oil of Olay Age Defying Series may or may not have fallen into my cart.

I met the Latino gentleman at a Capoeira event last year—four years into his curse. He approached me with an expression of surprise.

"You're aging much better than I expected," he said.

And, again, rather than kneeing him in the groin and hoping my shot landed wherever he hid his Polly Pocket-packaged man parts, I just smiled, as if I were ever so appreciative of his ill-advised encouragement. I may have been expiring, but I wasn't sour milk quite yet. Plus, we were sparring next, and the top of my foot was starting to tickle.

*For fear that an angry pack of twenty something crones with fury and a whisper of crow's feet might storm the "Latino gentleman's" house, I will not reveal his name. No I won't. No way, Jose.

Shadow, At Your Service

Our dog believes he is hired help.

Shadow, our grey cockapoo with curly hair, a bushy mustache, and sweet eyes, was lying on the grass in the sun, chin resting on paws and legs splayed like a frog, contorted in that way he finds most comfortable. I needed a break from work, so I went outside for some fresh air. As soon as I stepped out onto the deck, he shot up from his resting pose, glanced at me guiltily, and began running around the yard, barking madly at everything.

I've seen that behavior before. In fact, I've behaved that way before. It's the reflex reaction of an employee trying to look occupied when the supervisor walks into the room. His lazing around is my scrolling through Facebook, and his barking wildly is my messing with papers on my desk. *Yup, nothing to see here, boss. Just yelping at trees and birds. You know, doing my job. You guys sure keep me busy around here. If you send me to the pound, you'd have a butt-load of extra patrolling the perimeter to do.*

This notion explains why Shadow is constantly switching between inside and outside—there's no better way to look busy than by rushing in and out of the office. Advice from a professional: it helps if you look especially anxious. To establish this effect, I speed walk and pump my arms. Shadow's version is wagging his tail and nudging the door with his nose.

I also now understand why Shadow feels the need

to greet everyone at the door; he's playing the part of a dutiful receptionist. And when he deems the visitor to be a particularly important client, he shows his respect, not by shaking his hand, but by sniffing his crotch, and not by bringing the individual a cup of coffee, but by collapsing at his feet and peeing.

On walks, Shadow obsessively marks his territory on trees, mailboxes, and leaves—even if he's got nothing left to mark with. Perhaps that's his idea of distributing his business card. He knows that, even if it's likely nothing will come of it, it never hurts to put your name out there.

Whenever Shadow is given the bones from our dinner, rather than enjoying them on the spot, he takes them directly outside and buries them. That's how I know Shadow is a responsible investor, and like an employer with a 401K, I feel more inclined to contribute to his future. And when Shadow runs away, I suppose he's cashing in on his vacation time.

Dog treats are, obviously, performance bonuses, and maybe dog parks are like canine conferences. A diverse group of breeds gather from all across the neighborhood for the alleged purpose of learning something new—but we all know you can't teach an old dog new tricks—so the true incentive is networking. The Yorkshires yap, the Chihuahuas chatter, and the Schnauzers schmooze. Every dog is there to mingle, sniff around for opportunities, and maybe kiss some ass.

When my previous dog dragged a deer leg out from the forest and dropped it at our door, maybe that was her idea of finishing up and turning in a report.

I wonder if Shadow likes his job. If he was dissatisfied with his work environment originally, he must be thrilled with recent company reorganization. Since my brothers and I moved out, our dog has enjoyed significant upward movement. Like his cubicle, for instance. His entry-level space was in a cage. Then, over time, he was promoted to the window seat, and then worked his way up to the couch. Since the change in corporate structure, Shadow has had his choice of offices, complete with beds and walls and windows with a view. His new position has really gotten to his head. I heard he's been rotating between all three of our bedrooms.

Now, when nobody is looking, he acts like he owns the place, lounging around on the couch or in the grass. But, I suppose, like a typical employee, he takes the breaks he's entitled to.

Costco: Or Why I Might Be On A Terrorist Watch List

Costco exhausts me. You know how the elderly have to distribute their obligations across an entire week (laundry on Tuesday, drugstore on Thursday, etc.) because everything is so damn tiring? That's how I am with Costco. I walk into that warehouse, and I'm not just wiped, I'm done for the day.

Management realizes the stamina required to get from hygiene to produce and then back up again to computer supplies—that's why they set up sample stands at every aisle. Those noble men and women in their red hats and aprons dispensing bites of dumplings or pizza bagels are as essential to the process as are the individuals handing out cups of water along marathon routes. And that, of course, makes me the runner. I'm bent at a forty five-degree angle in order to push the oversized cart, which by the time I reach the cereal section is already piled with tubs of shampoo and conditioner; 1,000 tablets of Tylenol; tampons fit to stock a women's prison; and enough toothpaste to trace a mint football field, complete with yard lines and a team logo. Setting my sights on the next table equipped with a mini oven and toothpicks is the only thing fueling me from section to section.

By the time I slump my way to the cashier, my cart is teeming—one sharp turn away from a wreck— but there's no getting around the sheer measure of product. There might be only four items in the carriage, but it's the quantity of those four items that demands such space. If I want to shave my legs, I have to buy 52 razors. When I walk out with that many blades, I know the cashier is wondering what manner of forestry I'm hiding under my cardigan. And their Parmesan cheese container has such a circumference that it requires two hands to hold. When I'm topping off my spaghetti, I feel like a baby gripping its bottle of milk. Costco sells 50% of the world's supply of cashews, and I'm fairly confident that's just in one container. Caskets may be the only item Costco sells in moderation, although I've honestly never looked into it. They very well might come in twelve-packs.

Despite what my local grocery bagger might think (every time I pull up to checkout, he says, "Big family, huh?"), I am part of a small household. The second smallest possible, actually. Two. Costco was not made for families like ours. The toilet paper I bought last year is still in reserves. We live in a one-bedroom apartment, and I have a roll of toilet paper in every cabinet, nook, and drawer. I find toilet paper rolls like parents discover rotten Easter eggs they forgot they hid.

Then there's the canola oil—my god—the canola oil. Olive oil is our oil of choice; it's what we use to sauté onions and garlic, which is the foundation for pretty much every meal. But, occasionally, I bake muffins, so when I spotted the industrial sized canola oil at Costco, I thought to myself, *That would be better for muffins.* And, without due process, I bought it. Do you know how many batches of banana walnut muffins I'll have to bake to get through that vat of oil? 320. That's over 2,000 muffins. Breakfast at my place?

And this is why I fear that I might be on a domestic terrorist watch list.

The FBI has labeled bulk food purchase (more than seven days worth) as potential terrorist activity, and God knows it's going to take more than a week for Phil and I to eat our way through three pounds of almonds.

I don't blame the Feds. I'll be the first to admit that my behavior is suspicious. What do I, a childless woman of 26, need with twelve pounds of peanut butter? The authorities would sooner assume that I'm improvising some manner of Skippy Super Chunky explosive device than believe we eat that much creamy protein by the spoonful to stave off hunger pains. (Government suspicion may be heightened by my recent Google search, "Can you make a bomb with peanut butter?" The scary thing is—somebody already asked that question on Wiki answers. The answer, it seems, is no, unless you mean the fun sweet treat by the name Peanut Butter Bomb.)

I can just see myself cordoned off in a small, stark room with nothing but a metal table and a spotlight, an agent sitting across from me, calmly chewing a peanut butter on white bread sandwich, waiting for me to break. I insist that we aren't terrorists; we just really enjoy peanut butter. We eat it on celery, soft bread, toasted bread, graham crackers, saltine crackers, pretzels of all shapes and sizes, apples, and even, simply, plain. Finally, he loses it. He snaps, pounding the table and jumping to his feet. "But twelve pounds of it? Cut the bull***t. Not even the Duggars need that amount of whipped nut. This is chemical warfare and we know it. You're going after the new wave of kids with peanut allergies, aren't you? Aren't you??"

The truth is, of course, that I don't need twelve pounds of peanut butter. Just like I don't need 25 lbs of potatoes, 500 Ziploc sandwich bags, 5 quarts of liquid plumber, 2,400 sheets of computer paper, 700 coffee filters, or 10 cans of water chestnuts. But I can't resist. I can't resist the idea of never having to shop for water chestnuts again, and I can't resist the suggestion that, by purchasing my year's supply of toilet paper upfront, I'm saving.

That is the allure. It's why Costco has 58 million members worldwide, and why its security is tighter than an airport. (They demand to see your membership card at the door, screen your receipt on your way out, and last week the cashier asked me for three forms of identification. "I do this to everybody," he assured me. But I didn't see him do it to the woman before me or the woman after me, so I think he's full of a Costco amount of baloney, and that I was a victim of age profiling.) It's why customers will put up with quirky eccentricities like only accepting American Express and, despite stocking boxes of 200 count kitchen garbage bags, that there is no plastic in sight at the end of checkout. After being fatigued by towers of goods, you now have to face lugging all of your purchases from cart to car and from car to home without the help of handles.

If this doesn't seem like a big deal, then you weren't in the parking lot watching me navigate a cart brimming with groceries when I hit a bump in the sidewalk. My clamshell of fresh raspberries slid off the top and exploded on the concrete below. The beautiful pink succulent raspberries that I was so looking forward to enjoying were everywhere, except in their plastic container. If Costco provided bags, that never would have happened.

Like I mentioned earlier, Costco exhausts me, so I was already skittering on the temperament of an infant in need of a nap, and this disaster was the mean older sister that pinches you when your mother turns her back. My eyes watered. My lip trembled. I abandoned my cart, ran back inside, and tugged on the sleeve of the first person I saw wearing a red apron.

"My raspberries," I said, trying to grip the last remaining shreds of composure. "They fell. And they rolled. And they are everywhere."

"Go get another one," she said, taking a step away from the crazy lady before I sobbed into her bosom.

So I did. I sprinted to the back produce area, grabbed the top box of raspberries in the stack, and walked back out of the store, carrying my prize like a lollipop.

As I approached my cart, sitting where I left it in the middle of the sidewalk, some astute man who surely must have been a private eye spotted my mess and smartly said, "Oops. Looks like somebody lost their raspberries." Ahh, I believe you are correct, my dear Watson. A very clever conjecture. It does seem as if somebody lost their raspberries. Idiot.

I slowed my pace so that he would pass before identifying me as the loser.

Although, being known as the woman who cried over spilt fruit is much less dangerous than being recognized as a person of interest. So, if you're reading, FBI, we are only criminal overeaters. Please don't lock me up. Even though a lot of this food doesn't expire for another year, it may take that long for me to get through it, and I just don't have any doing-time to spare.

If Nobody Sees My Apartment, Do I Still Have to Clean It?

Cleaning is a gigantic drag. For every stroke of the broom, I can come up with another life obligation I'd rather be doing. Having an oil change. Paying my bills. Getting a physical. And this isn't because I'm obsessed with my car or have tons of money or a hot doctor (D: None of the above). It's because dusting and sweeping and scrubbing away the filth that accumulates in every nook and cranny of our one-bedroom apartment displeases me. Mucho.

First, it's gross. Have you ever let your house get to the point that the dust climbs the walls as if bitten by a radioactive arachnid? Believe me, it happens. Dust seems harmless when isolated to just a few specks, but when allowed to form a united front, it's nasty. Especially in the corners. I approach corners as if I'm expecting to find an assailant tucked behind the dressers. And when I pull the furniture aside to expose the neglected crooks, what I discover is ghastly. The dust has slowly, silently been gathering force. After three months (okay, six months...maybe a year) of disregard, it becomes an alien mass. A grey ball-shaped monster, woven together with the threads of our filth. And it's quick. I come at it with a broom and it darts away, rolling with the speed of a pool ball shooting toward a pocket. To eliminate these creatures, you must sneak up on them. No sudden movements. And no fear.

They can smell your fear. Fear was how they formed in the first place.

The second cause of my disdain is that cleaning makes me sneeze. And sneezing makes my eyes water and my mouth itch. So just when I extricate the dust from its hiding places so that it's flurrying out in the open, I abandon my task to lie on the couch in snotty, soggy, scratchy misery.

Third, I get nasty sneers every time I go onto our back deck and bang the dust out of the broom. Maybe that's because our neighbors are within arm's length and the clumps of dust float directly from my broom to their faces, but, come on, since when did a little dust in the face warrant a sneer?

I can hear my mother preaching something like, "Well that's why they call it a chore. If it was fun, they'd call it doing your plays." But what annoys me most about cleaning the apartment is not the activity itself (although it really is no fun) but the futility of it all, because by the time I replace the sponge and Comet back under the sink and tuck the broom back in its corner, I turn around and can practically see fresh dust settling on the room. I don't know where it comes from, but it reproduces like Catholics.

Which makes me ask myself: Why do it in the first place? I still maintain my eight-year-old mentality of "Why waste time and effort making the bed if I'm just going to sleep in it again tonight?" It's a fair question.

Yes, I get that it's not socially acceptable to be knee deep in dust bunnies, and when we eventually do have offspring, we certainly don't want to be the house that the other children aren't allowed to visit. But right now we not only don't have kids, we don't have friends.

Phil and I aren't outcasts. We just moved away from everybody we know and our efforts to meet people have been...noncommittal. We did join a volleyball league and an Italian cooking class, but we found that the main audience interested in adult education opportunities at the local high school is middle-aged women who are bored by their partners. After the sixth woman reminded me how lucky I am that my husband still wants to spend time with me, we decided that we were mingling with the wrong demographic. And instead of pouring our energies into something more appropriate, we quit. Okay, maybe it's our own fault, but how do you meet new people? Are there pickup lines to feed potential buddies at bars? And what if we still like our old friends? Maybe the root of the issue is that, subconsciously, we believe that if we build new friendships in Long Island, we are resigning ourselves to staying here, and that is not something we are willing to accept yet. We may be tired of trying to leave, but we have not yet surrendered. The battle is lost, but the war is ours, damn it. Anyway...

In the year and a half that we've had this apartment, it has seen people other than ourselves on only ten occasions, and one of those occasions was when our Internet wasn't working, so the Cablevision guy was getting paid to be there.

So, who am I cleaning for? From what I can tell, Phil doesn't notice that the apartment needs a cleaning until the dust bunnies are so substantial that a breeze skitters them across the hardwood floor like tumbleweed in a Western flick, and you can almost hear the whistling wind and Spanish guitar in the background.

I once engaged him in a rousing game of cleaning chicken. I had been the one to clean the last several times and was determined to hold out until he initiated. But he was good. Boy, was he good. Coffee grounds scattered on the kitchen floor and he pretended not to notice. We tracked sand in from the beach and he feigned ignorance. I couldn't compete with such expert nonchalance. I broke down when our living quarters got to the point that the dirt washed off my feet in the shower and made mud.

"Fine, that's it. You win. I'll clean!" I said.

Phil looked genuinely surprised, as if he didn't

even realize we were dueling. "Why, is the apartment dirty?"

That's why I wonder if I even have to clean at all. It's like the question of the tree falling in the forest—if nobody sees that my apartment is a sty, am I dirty? Or can I still behave like a cleanly person without anybody knowing the difference? People have had more scandalous secrets. For instance, I knew a woman for years before unearthing that she was afraid of zippers. Okay, maybe that's not scandalous per say, but it sure is weird.

I keep my cool when discussing household cleanliness. (Such social dialogue doesn't happen often, but sometimes conversation does get slow.) When one of my friends mentions that she changes her towels after every use, I nod politely; I don't pound my chest and bellow my true feelings—that it's a ridiculous and wasteful practice since the towel just dried a freshly washed body, so why the hell does it need to be laundered every single time? Is your body that pock-ridden that even directly following a soap, suds, and rinse, still nothing can touch you without then being sanitized?

Because I play the part of a moderately unsoiled citizen, our friends will never suspect that our shopping list could be written in the dust layer on top of our bookcase. It may be true, but they will never find out. I will not let them.

Weight Loss Methods I Wish Worked

Lying down is one of my favorite pastimes.

Because of this preference for passiveness, it's very difficult for me to workout. Why move around, sweat, and increase my heart rate when I can curl up on my bed and...not? I don't just enjoy lying down, I'm good at it, and like I learned from the biblical story my mother so often referenced when trying to motivate (guilt) me into practicing the piano, I shouldn't bury my talents.

Sadly, every three months or so, against my will, my pants tighten. Jeans are difficult to reason with—they don't respect my passion for lethargy—so I am forced to abandon my life's love, push myself out of bed, dust off my workout DVDs, and commence the squatting.

I look at an iPad or an origami swan and am reminded of all the amazing things my fellow humans have accomplished. And yet nobody has figured out how to stay slender without the inconvenience of getting up. Has no engineer ever been as drowsy as I am while still wanting to shake her fist at these injustices without her arm flab getting in the spirit?

Sure, there have been attempts, and I appreciate them because every failed trial gets us one (metaphoric) step closer to maintaining a six-pack while drinking one.

Here are a few unsuccessful methods that have disappointed me:

The Ab Belt:

Strap on this belly blaster and zap your stomach into submission without ever having to voluntarily flex a muscle. Equipped with 30 settings ranging from static electricity to electric chair, this core stimulator gives you the extra jolt you never knew you never wanted. Plus, it makes the ideal birthday present if you're looking to end a friendship.

This was the most painful $50 plus shipping my parents ever spent. At least I thought so. I returned during a college break to find my mom and dad sitting on the couch watching *Everybody Loves Raymond* while passing this electro strap-on back and forth.

"What are doing?" I asked.

"Working out!" my mother said.

Upon hearing that this device crunches your stomach while you kick back with a bag of chips, I plopped down in line. I now know what it feels like to resist arrest, as my parents set their Ab Belt to Taser.

It felt like I was a Berkeley rioter alone in a room with roided out police officers. The electric needles stabbed my stomach in an angry synchronized beat.

I yelped and my mother said, "Yeah, you have to build a resistance to the pain. We started at a low setting and worked our way up."

Thanks, Mom, for information that would have been helpful before I belted on that violence.

As I struggled to pull off the belt that was punishing me for a crime I never committed, my thumbs throbbed as if I'd stuck them in an electric socket.

"Oh, and your hands aren't supposed to touch it while it's on."

She was two for two.

That was the last time I subjected myself to this torture regimen, but the fact that I haven't heard its rhythmic buzz around my parents' house in eight years suggests that it only left their abs worse for wear.

I wonder if my mother donated the Ab Belt to Goodwill and its malice is currently circulating around the pudgy middles of Fairfield County, or if it's boxed up somewhere in the attic, just waiting until enough time has passed that we've forgotten the pain, and will give this fiend another chance.

The Frozen Food Fat Froster:

Freeze out your blubber because fat cells are like New England seniors: once it gets too cold, they travel down south. This method is inspired by Cryolipolysis (the medical procedure popularly known as Cool Sculpting, which dissolves fat cells using laser, ultrasound, or rf current at very low temperatures), but The Frozen Food Fat Froster is designed for huskies on a budget. Why pay thousands of dollars to a plastic surgeon when you can simply shop at your local grocer?

How it works: Hold frozen food against those problem areas. Flabby butt? Shove a bag of corn into your underwear. Paunchy stomach? Defrost your dinner meat against that tubby tummy. This should yield the same results as the medical method, proving there's no need for laser, ultrasound, or rf current when you stock your freezer with peas, steak, and ravioli. Plus, after the food reaches room temperature, you can eat it—guilt free! (Insider's tip: Unless you want your new slender shape to have frostbite, wrap your food item in paper towel).

I can't take credit for the invention of this process. I gleaned it from my mother who, after reading an advertisement for the plastic surgery, walked around the house with a pack of frozen hot dogs tucked into the front of her waistband, proving that: When you're working on your appearance, you can't worry about appearances.

I suppose I should mention that, if you are too

good to wear frozen food in your pants (ahem, pretentious), you could purchase the FreezeAwayFat Cool Shape Shorts with cold gel inserts. Same concept with a higher price tag, albeit a lower rate of humiliation. But the frozen food method is patented by the Dillons so, who do you trust—a corporation informed by NASA scientists or a desperate suburban family? I'd bet those NASA scientists are in terrific shape, and have never even had to lie on their beds to zip up jeans. Therefore, who are the real weight loss experts?

I think your answer is clear. Just remember: when your skin tingles with freezer burn, that's when you know it's working!

The Diet Fork:

With its short, dulled teeth, small shape, and uncomfortable grip, this fork is actually the anti-fork, engineered to inhibit eating. For the irresistible price of $10 for 10, you too can make eating a struggle. Alternatives include eating soup with a regular fork, or spaghetti with a spoon. (Caution: For the hungry dieter, this method may result in dropping the fork and eating like a starving Pit Bull.)

I understand the concept here but maintain that if the Japanese can eat using only two sticks and still produce men worthy of sumo wrestling, a short fork would slow me down only initially. I would overcome.

Weight Loss Earrings:

Get thin through fashion with these aesthetically pleasing ear magnets. Place on your lobe one hour prior to meals, and keep them on as long as you can stand "the pinch." For those who believe in pressure point therapy, that's the design of these magnets. For those who believe in aversion therapy, that's the design of these magnets. For those who believe in God, that's the design of these magnets. Just order them, okay?

Earrings, for weight loss. Pain, for weight loss. I

have no comment to add.

My point here is this: while I appreciate the feeble efforts made thus far to aid lazy people through their plight of losing weight without losing their slothful identities, we are only just beginning. These methods are the Z1 Computers of the weight loss technology revolution, and what I'm interested in is the MacBook Pros. I want our finest minds to set aside their next great vaccine initiative and concentrate on conceiving The Fat Zapper Laser Handset—a wand designed to locate and disintegrate fat cells on command—the innovation that will allow us to look back and laugh at such elementary devices as The Ab Belt, or at least allow those who aren't already laughing about it.

Once this is accomplished, scientists can begin on my next modernization: an effort to eliminate the inconveniences of pregnancy while still propelling the human race...

Oh, yes. The external womb.

The Heartache of a TV Serial Dater

Finishing a television series feels like the end of a relationship. There's that same dull ache in your chest, knowing that the characters aren't part of your life anymore. No more late nights lying on the couch together after a long day. No more shared adventures. All that's left are your memories and reruns.

Last night, *24* and I concluded things once and for all. Over. Finale. It probably should have ended at least a season earlier, when Jack started hanging out with guys like Freddy Prinze Jr. with his fake New York accent that didn't crop up until episode two, but it seems that all serious relationships never end as soon as they should. It's too hard to say goodbye, so it gets renewed for another year.

Although I saw our breakup coming for a while, it was still every bit as difficult as I expected it would be. I believe it's for the best since I probably sacrificed too much of my life just to spend time at home with Jack, but I will miss his mysterious darkness, his insufferable angst, and his devotion to his country. I know he could never have been truly happy while we were together; he felt too much pressure to perform. But maybe now that we're apart, he can remember how to just be himself.

After the closing scene, when the laptop screen went black and, in the silence, I prepared to deal with my emotions, my husband turned to me and said, "So, what now? Want to try *Bones*?"

What a typical man. He didn't need time to

recover. The credits hadn't even finished rolling and he was ready to start on the next series. I'm surprised he didn't go ahead and suggest *Rome*, since what he really wanted was some action.

But I wasn't ready to start something new, to barrel through those first couple of episodes where you're just getting to know the characters, learning their names, their sense of humor, and their bad habits. It can be clumsy and uncomfortable, and if I begin a new series before I'm fully over the last one, I revert back to the faces I've grown to love. My nostalgia takes over. I'd go back to Jack, hoping it would be like it was. But of course, reruns never are.

Don't get me wrong, I know there will be other shows, but it's still too soon. They say it takes half the length of a relationship to really get over it so, since *24* was eight seasons of twenty-four hours, I think I at least deserve to mourn for four days—four days where I just take time off from the whole television thing and really concentrate on my own life. Take long baths, do yoga, cook. It's during this space that I'll process the show, examine Jack's character arc, the mistakes he made, and yes, I'll remember the good times too. I know I'll want to reach out to Jack, maybe re-watch the series premiere, but I'll resist. It's crucial to have a clean break. Eventually, I'll reach closure, and maybe consider *The Closer*.

But first I'll need a rebound show—probably some shallow sitcom that everybody has watched—trust me, right now, I don't need drama—and then maybe after a few episode flings, I'll be ready to begin something steady. Even when there is another protagonist in my life, Jack will always have a special place in my heart.

This is probably my most painful TV breakup. I thought splitting up with *Lost* was going to destroy me, but, toward the end, it just didn't satisfy me anymore. Nothing so complicated could have ended smoothly; it had made more promises than it could keep. The main reason for my disappointment, of course, was that, in retrospect, *Lost* was never what I thought it was. There are still fond memories, though: the desperation for our next meeting, the constant surprises, and the existential examinations. The truth is, it's better to have loved *Lost* than to never have loved at all.

The Sopranos ending allowed for zero closure, so I just jumped blindly into *True Blood*, but that was a mistake and didn't work out because it was into some dark things...sexually. It ended after only one episode.

Friends was true love. It was always so comforting and easy. We lounged and laughed for ten good years. Sometimes we cried, but then Monica would put on her fat suit or Joey would eat an entire pizza, and we laughed again. I just couldn't let it end, so I made an exception and bought the series on DVD. Only in this case could I settle for *Friends* with benefits.

Losing *Prison Break* was pretty ugly because Michael Schofield died (rest in peace), and so unexpectedly. On the other hand, maybe that helped me move on, knowing there was no way we could have stayed together for another season. Against all odds, Jack Bauer didn't die. He chose to leave. Even though it was for his own good, that's still difficult to accept.

This was also the longest relationship I've ever had with a series. I think the hardest part will be finding ways to fill the time we spent together. I hope it rains later, so I can perch at my window and gaze out at the storm longingly, wondering where Jack is and what he's doing. Does he finally have enough time? If not, do people at least appreciate the rush he is in? Tonight I'll probably lean on my *Friends* and eat half a gallon of frozen yogurt straight out of the carton. Hey, it's my right. I'm going through a breakup.

Agony of DeFeet

Pedicures are the last remaining form of acceptable modern day slavery. I'm not saying this because there are cases of importing women for the sole purpose (no pun intended) of working at salons (although there are, and that's terrible), but because having to touch strangers' feet all day long is not just disgusting, it feels unethical.

There are no regulations for quality of feet. No matter what manner of atrocity is flexed in their face, pedicurists can't point to an official diagram framed on their walls and say, "Sorry, that foot is just not up to code. We can't service you here." They just have to fill that mini tub full of water and take a deep breath (and in particularly smelly cases, put on a paper mask). I know this because, without hesitation, they've washed, scrubbed, rubbed, and painted my hooves while I sat up on my cushy, electric massage chair throne flipping through the latest issue of Vogue (or worse, chatting on my cell phone). I never feel so elitist as when I'm looking down at a person whose fingers are between my toes.

I used to train a martial art five times a week on floors of hardwood, concrete, grass, and/or cement. This routine meant that number one, I was once in great shape and, number two, my feet grew a pair of skin socks. In addition to all varieties of blisters, I had calluses thick enough to walk across molten coals.

Did that prevent the heroines at Fantasy Fingers from inviting me into their chairs? No, it didn't. Sure, while they filed down my hobbit pads, they pointed to abscesses, grimaced, and sometimes made a sign of the cross, but I've had friends who saw my feet and dry-heaved, so I was impressed by the discretion of those professionals.

True, this is not a free favor, so perhaps slavery is not the most accurate choice of words. But, I will say this, the amount of money you'd have to pay me to kneel in front of a grab-bag pair of dogs, pull off the socks, and get elbow deep in foreign toe grime, is not $25.

Although, if I was taking advantage of their services, they got theirs too. Every time I walked into a spa and one of the ladies looked up to greet me, her expression would drop into one of sympathy. She'd point to her own forehead and say, knowingly, "You're here for eyebrow wax?"

And I was never there for eyebrow wax.

Section III

True Imaginings

The Largest Magazine in the World is No Place for the Likes of Me

Dear Writer (although we both know I'm being wildly generous with that title),

Certainly you are aware that *Haughty* is the largest magazine in the world, so we must assume that your submission was a mistake, a mere slip of the finger, a twitch you really should get checked out. You see, you are nothing but a crumb on our plates. You are lint in our interns' belly buttons. You are a stranger's hair clung to this season's Michael Kors pea coat due to the torments of static electricity in winter months.

But, in the laughable unlikelihood that you in fact intended to contact us in regards to your attempt at a humorous essay, actually expecting us to consider it, I'm here to inform you, and then reiterate, that *Haughty* is the largest magazine in the world. Not large. Or larger. But largest. Capiche? Excuse me, Italian isn't sophisticated enough of a language for us here at *Haughty*. Allow me to rephrase: Comprenez-vous? Ugh, excuse me again. That was the formal conjugation, but there's no need for such linguistic respect on my part given that I hold the coveted position of Staff Member at *Haughty* magazine and you are a peon who will never see her name reflected back off of *Haughty*'s glossy pages so, one last time: tu comprends?

Haughty does not consider itself a starting point

for writers, nor those just learning to read (which, if I'm not mistaken, is your case, no?). *Haughty* considers itself, in addition to being the largest magazine in the world, the pinnacle of a writer's career. We are a snowcapped apex glittering (out of your reach) at sunset. Yes, we are the starving artist's Everest. That's why our unofficial motto is, "It's all downhill from *Haughty*." When a reader opens *Haughty*, she expects the pages to radiate with esteemed names such as Dior, Prada, and E.L James. She doesn't expect, well.... you, a high school dropout with more time than a Rolex—although that's just an educated guess.

We are a revered periodical, tackling important topics like: *10 Easy Ways to Look Easy*; *How to Change Everything About You so You Aren't Such a Lame Loser*; and *Sex: What Goes Where*. Whatever the issue, *Haughty* is here to help. We'd be a nonprofit organization if we didn't also enjoy making so much money.

You, writer, are probably thinking, "Well if you're so philanthropic, why are you rejecting me?" All I can say to that is, if you're looking for a miracle worker, go find Anne Sullivan.

May we at *Haughty* recommend a more appropriate placement for your jocular yarns? Perhaps email it to a friend, or read it aloud to your grandmother (assuming your friend has your email address flagged as spam and your grandmother is either deaf or senile). Or print it, shred it, and use it as mulch. Or donate it to your local Girl Scout Troop as kindling for earning their Camp Fire merit badges. At the very least, use it as a reminder not to quit your part time job, which I presume includes standing outside a McDonald's dressed as the Hamburglar waving a desperate invitation in the form of a stuffed pickle.

We deduce that this is the first piece of writing you've ever read that doesn't end, "And they all lived happily ever after." Well, writer, it's time to put on your big girl pants—and for a pair that will make your ass look less like a deflated balloon, pick up our September issue.

Eternally yours and the rest of society's favorite and largest publication,
Haughty

On Taking My Love Affair with a Friendly's Reese's Peanut Butter Cup Friend-Z to the Next Level

I, Alena, take you, Reese's Peanut Butter Cup Friend-Z, to be my one true vice. I will cherish the velvety delight of your peanut butter topping, letting its thick gooeyness coat my tongue like a passionate embrace alive with flavor and adoration. I will honor your creamy vanilla soft-serve, loving it more and more each minute it melts. Your hot fudge is like water on parched lips, if water is chocolate and parched lips are my gluttonous cravings. And, when spooning the beautiful swirling union of your ingredients into my mouth, I stumble upon a peanut butter cup chunk, I will treasure the good fortune, for I realize how blessed I am. Not everybody is lucky enough to have found their soul-munch. Friend-Z, you make me a bigger person.

I know you have flaws. The state of New York has many times over warned me of your 860 calories per serving. But to the state I ask, "What is a spare tire compared to the limitless joy and all-consuming rapture?" Yes, I may be padded, but it is not just with fat, but also with happiness. Nobody appreciates you as a source of calcium and protein like I do, and nothing compares to the pure contentedness of not just having found my love, but my best Friend-Z.

So, Friendly's Reese's Peanut Butter Cup Friend-Z, I vow to laugh and cry over you today, tomorrow, and forever. I will savor you alone, eating you faithfully, through sickness and in health, in good times and in bad times. When life is easy, I will celebrate with you. When life is difficult, you alone will feed my feelings, for you are my one true comfort food. What may come, you will always be there. As long as there is a Friendly's within a ten-mile radius, and I can scrape together $4.35, I intend to hold you in my hand, so help me God. I do.

Buy My Crap—It's for Charity!

I'm not a monster or a Scrooge. I care about the well-being of inner-city children. I don't want them to become drug dealers or to join gangs. I want them to succeed. So, Neighborhood Teen, thank you for coming to our doorstep and engaging us in a conversation about a worthwhile issue. Alas, I'm giving you squat. The reason I'm going to decline purchasing any items from your warped sauce-stained Tupperware container is not that I don't believe in your cause. It's that I don't believe in you. No offense.

Verbally, you've got the gig down pat. You delivered your speech with the appropriate level of solemnity, and you nailed all of the buzzwords. You even used "youth" instead of "kids." For that, I respect your efforts. But you can't tell me that the contents of your ratty plastic bowl were supplied by a legitimate charity organization. I have incidentals in my junk drawer that look more salable than your motley crew of a selection: a votive candle, a bar of peanut brittle, a silver pen, and hand sanitizer. This is what the Fresh Air Fund provided? Don't make me laugh in your face. That would be rude. Friend, I've previously donated to your organization, and the spokesperson before you carried a sturdy box stuffed with Snickers and Skittles. That's right, multiple products of the same brand. A uniform display. And, guess what. He was asking for two dollars per candy. Reasonable. I bought five and felt good about my generous self, my investment, and the chocolate melting in my mouth. You expect me to hand over ten dollars for a wick in a thimble of wax that you probably just lifted off of your mother's coffee table? You say it's lavender scented? I say it smells like a scam. I don't need a smart phone to be hip to your game.

Let me tell you something. Phil, the young man who answered the door together with our landlord (the older gentleman wearing the armpit-stained white t-shirt who saw you, said, "I don't have a job," turned around, and walked into his apartment—probably to return to work) is a generous guy. I've seen him hand a subway beggar a $20 bill for no reason other than that she asked for it. If he looked at your assorted goods with incredulity, you've got yourself a real presentation problem. You're lucky he answered the door instead of me. He's nice. He handed you three bucks and wished you well. If it had been me, I wouldn't have funded your sham. At best, I would have invited you upstairs to restock your inventory out of our junk drawer. You know what would have looked appealing lying next to your dollar store treasures? Cherry flavored cough drops, hot chocolate packets, a lighter, a San Francisco key chain, and a Tide stick—only used twice! You know what, I'm starting to feel a little more philanthropic. Go ahead and take our loose change too. If you're hocking your trash for 10 dollars each, you might as well try to shine up a quarter and peddle it at the same price point.

I don't know what you need the money for. New sneakers? A birthday gift for your girlfriend? Beer? Whatever the cause truly is, I swear to you, you'd be better off with honesty. Something like, "Neighbor, I want a video game, so I rounded this crap up from around my house. Would you care to buy miscellaneous garbage to help me reach my goal?"

I have to admit that you've got yourself an innovative idea. You just need to launch a new marketing plan. Ditch the deceit and call it what it is. Maybe Paul's Porch Pawn Shop or Timmy's Traveling

Tag Sale (If your name is neither Paul nor Timmy, these are far more forgivable frauds than claiming that the money is going to save needy children from a life of crime). I can't speak for the other residents of our block but, as for me, I'd sooner support a young entrepreneur than an aspiring conman. Good day!

A Study of the Habits and Identities of Native Long Islanders From the Perspective of Somebody Who is Only Here Temporarily. Seriously. We're Leaving Soon.

Despite the protests of my colleagues, I decided that the only authentic method for truly understanding the workings of Long Island culture was to immerse myself in it—to live amongst them. I was told that it was too dangerous, that the risks weren't even worth the potential findings. My peers feared that, if I could not escape, I would be forced to bare children in this foreign land and that my own offspring would become one of the strange specimens I sought to study. It was a valid worry. Now, as I begin my third year inside this mysteriously proud civilization, I admit that I'm more afraid than ever.

Alas, I am here. What is done cannot be undone. In the following paper, I will share what I have come to learn thus far, for better or worse. No, wait: it's a perfectly sunny day out and yet I'm currently watching a native dry his car using a leaf blower. I'm here definitely for worse.

I still haven't determined if the natives are aware of life outside the island. They consider "going away" commuting from the south shore to the north shore, and when I mention the bridges, they hiss. Upon further investigation in the form of interviews, I was told things like, "Why would I ever leave when Long Island has everything?" or, "No, I leave all the time. I visited a friend in Queens just last year." As a result of this reluctance to explore, inhabitants often reside on the same block as their extended family. This close association with family members might explain the proclivity for mobs. Or, in the case of the five people on Long Island who are not of Italian ancestry, gangs.

Along the same vein, children seem disinclined to move out of their parents' houses, often living comfortably in their childhood rooms until they approach thirty years old. Interviews on this subject yielded responses like, "Why would I move out? Then I'd have to pay rent."

The most profound difference between this tribe and my own is evident in dialect. From their witness alone, one would think they've named their home Lawn Guyland, but from prior knowledge, I know this to be a bastardization of two English words: Long and Island. This name is quite accurate; days on the island are seemingly endless, and the island is physically long enough to span a variety of habitats, ranging from farm to practically urban. (Additional note on dialect: no word here ends in "er". For example, "explorer" and "loser" become "explorah" and "losah.")

The mating behaviors of females are peculiar. Every partial thought is punctuated by "like" and "oh my gawd." They attach colored plastic claws to their hands, wear a second skin of velour fabric, and totter about on spiked footwear. The males are just as attentive in their grooming. It seems that the amount of hair product an individual uses is in direct correlation with his desire to procreate.

I must assume that the locals have an inherently poor sense of direction—why else would all of the streets, from tip to tip and shore to shore, be straight. I wonder if their aversion to turns is socially or genetically induced.

The straight, flat streets (also called parkways, routes, highways, avenues, expressways, turnpikes, and roads—all with multiple lanes and street lights) are lined with shopping plazas, each equipped with a pizza place, nail salon, bagel shop, and tattoo parlor, leading me to believe that they are sustained primarily by dough and culturally motivated by artificial body coloring.

The entire ecosystem is like one giant, concrete, open-air shopping center with houses; it isn't much more than a network of highways lined with outdoor malls connecting indoor malls. In Long Island, the highway circuit seems as revered as former presidents, as they've named public schools after both: Northern Parkway Elementary School and Barack Obama Elementary School are in the same county. The implication of this observation is, as of yet, inconclusive.

I have not yet established what occupies their days (besides shopping and getting tattoos). There are many cars on the streets—traffic as far as the eye can see. But because I've noted from previous research that they are not leaving the island, I cannot imagine where they are so eager to travel. Tangah Outlets? New Yawk City? No, it can't be the city because, although the natives refer to themselves as New Yawkers, they only go to New York City on rare occasions to see the Knicks play.

Through my limited contact with those outside the island, and through my extensive interactions with Long Island natives, I've observed an indisputable, but likewise inexplicable, hostility between Long Island and New Jersey aborigines. This reality perplexes me, as the two civilizations are almost indistinguishable: Their main sources of pride, and rightly so, are their beaches and their Italian food; they're both commutable to New York City and therefore (perhaps inaccurately) associate their identities with Manhattan; the lifestyles of their citizens range from the incredibly wealthy (Hamptons and Morris County) to the impoverished (Brentwood and Camden); the severity of their accents are linked to the residents' distance to the 718 area code; they are separated by bridges that no mainlander wants to cross; and they both have produced 60's pop-rock stars who are still performing long after they've lost their natural hairline.

As far as how this anthropological plunge has affected me, well, I miss life on the outside. Sometimes I forget what a mountain looks like, or how to drive without ever pressing on the horn and shouting, "Hey, asshole! You think you own the road?"

If I had known that this study would leave us stranded on this island for as long as it has, I never would have... oh, never mind. It's futile to think about that now.

We've managed to resist the ways of the island so far, but I pray to receive funding for a study elsewhere; I'm not sure how much longer we can hold on.

Letter from my Italian Landlord

"The staircase may not have railings. Live your vacation with some sense of adventure, just as we live our lives every day."
– The company from which we rented an Italian villa in Sorrento

Dear Guest,

Thank you for selecting Villa TheresBetter for your family vacation. Given your choice of hotels, motels, hostels, trailer parks, campsites, and alleyways, we are honored, and a bit surprised, that you selected Villa TheresBetter. Nevertheless, we are 70% confident that you will not regret making this reservation. Maybe 60%. But since we've already received and processed your deposit, and since you obviously aren't high rollers considering that you chose this destination above the many exceptionally rated accommodations easily found using a simple Google search, we are 100% confident that you will be coming even after reading this letter. Remember, you gave us your home address.

Please allow us to provide you with a few tips for surviving, I mean, improving, your experience at Villa TB.
• Be sure to bring matches, as our electricity is, shall we say, quirky.
• You prefer cold showers, right? They're good for your skin, as is showering fully clothed.

- Are you allergic to raccoons? If so, plan accordingly because they are territorial creatures and are living comfortably in our kitchen. Speaking of which, I assume you've had your rabies vaccine?
- The bed sheets are really just for show, so it would be favorable if you brought your own sleeping bag. But, if you insist on sleeping between our sheets, pack antibiotics. You know what, pack them in any case. Better to be safe than infected.
- Do you have a gun license? If not, this is something to consider. If this is impossible to obtain before your trip, don't worry; you'll probably be fine with a switchblade.
- If any of the "neighbors" come to "welcome you," just give them what they want.
- You may notice a cordoned off room with a door that seems to be continually slammed by the body of a creature estimated to be the size of a small grizzly. We ask that you use common sense. Don't open this door. It's a creature the size of a small grizzly.
- And, as a general rule, be alert: have a bag packed and ready to go, and always be aware of the quickest exit routes.

For your convenience, here are directions to the villa:

Once you get off the train, walk three blocks south until you see Mario. You'll know who Mario is because he'll be in a black trench coat and because he's the only person crazy enough to stand on the streets out in the open (and the only person crazy enough to wear a black trench coat in the heat of Italian summers. If nothing else, this trip will prepare you for Hell!). Give him our name; he'll know what to do. You may also want to give him money. This is recommended, unless you feel like you have too many fingers anyway. Continue for about a half-mile in the direction he points you. Pass the abandoned warehouses and smoking cars. Watch out for the discarded needles and used condoms.

We're the structure riddled with bullet holes, across the street from the crack house and adjacent to the brothel. If you start seeing nice houses, you've gone too far. Way too far.

When you're confident that you are standing outside the building, lie down. Yes, on the ground. Ever played possum? The goal here is to look as collapsed as possible. Bleeding would help, but curling up beside an actual dead person would be ideal. There should be plenty of those lying around on your route to the villa so, when you stumble over one, just drag it with you for the rest of the way.

Whatever you do, don't go directly inside uninvited. When we're ready, we'll come out to get you. The signal for your check-in will be when one of our personnel comes out to where you are playing dead and kicks you three times. Not twice. Not four times. Three times.

We encourage you to think of this as a taste of Italian culture—if Italy were a third world country during wartime. If you regret not having visited Kuwait in the early 90s, this is your chance to replicate that experience as authentically as possible.

We look forward to having you, even if you don't look forward to being had.

Sincerely,
The TB Team
PS. On the bright side, this location offers a lovely beach just a plane ride away!

Letter to Shameless Hurricane Relief Donors

Please note that we are no longer taking clothing or bedding, unless they are new and in original packaging.
– Excerpt from a Hurricane Sandy Relief organization email sent the day after I donated clothing and bedding NOT in original packaging

Dear Cause Contributors, Good and Bad:

First, please allow us to thank the many who donated generously, the ones who understand that people who have lost everything haven't necessarily lost their standards. These are the vacuum-sealed, rip-free, tag-still-on donors. My kind of donors.

We've happily received an abundance of quality nonperishable food, like canned goods that were not Stop and Shop, Food Club, or Great Value brands but epicurean varieties like Del Monte, Contadina, and Rich Dish. If I know this class of philanthropists, and I think I do, I bet these items weren't even purchased on sale. Our shelves are now stocked with Sumatra coffee beans, caviar, and Swiss chocolates—and not that mass produced Toblerone log that litters every airport across the country including the likes of Newark, NJ, but handmade truffles taken from the mouth of Svens and given to those in true need of the finest refined cacao. Your charity has been overwhelming and delicious.

Thanks for tightening your belt (and loosening mine!).

I'm thrilled to report that the kindness didn't stop at gourmet cuisine. Clothing, also, has been shipped in by the garment bags. The designer labels pop from collars, and I know these pieces didn't originate from the sale racks of Marshall's or T.J. Maxx because they just don't have that stale discount smell.

In addition to clothes, we've received a multitude of goodies. Merino wool blankets. Precious gemstone jewelry. Electronics (Apple, obviously). Some altruist even donated a week at their Newport Beach timeshare. Who's to say that this patron didn't intend his/her donation as a reward to a fellow Samaritan, which is why I will be unavailable next week. On a completely unrelated note, our organization is in dire need of frequent flyer miles.

For all of the aforementioned donations, we are appreciative. And if you were among this highbrow pedigree of benefactors, a thousand thank yous—you may ignore the remainder of this memo. However, if the above items sound unfamiliar, please, read on. Carefully.

When we say we need food, we do not mean leftovers from last night's dinner at the Olive Garden; milk that's about to expire; your box of matzah that is old enough to be Bar Mitzvahed; or a dusty can of clam chowder that you found in the back of your cabinet when you moved in. Here's a good policy: if you wouldn't eat it, don't donate it—throw it away. Here's another: if you can't use it, don't pawn it off on us. We're trying to accommodate thousands of displaced residents. What do you expect us to do with those mini ears of corn that nobody eats at salad bars? And what the hell is tahini?

I realize we stated an urgency for blankets. Apparently we should have been more specific. Anything you deem appropriate to deliver inside a Hefty garbage bag should probably just stay there. To be more specific, we don't need the afghan from when you lived in a basement apartment that was more humid than

Houston, Texas during a summer rodeo. It reeked and, just so you know, the volunteer who opened that bag now has asthma. You can also keep the Walmart blanket that's covered in cat hair; judging from the sheer volume of fur, Fluffy might need some back. What is that fabric, anyway? A polyester blend? Shiver. And, to the individual who donated that reversible comforter: forest green paired with maroon? Sorry, we don't want it. Nobody is *that* homeless.

As far as clothing and purses go, do us a favor and leave your knock-offs at home. Maybe they would be appropriate for a Halloween costume. You know, if you ever plan to dress up as a hooker. And when we said we would accept lightly worn articles, we assumed it'd be understood that this did not include baby items. Babies never wear clothing lightly. We have a stack of onesies so stained with spit up and other unmentionable body fluids, I can see the belly button imprint of the wailing baby they were peeled from. I'm beginning to gag just thinking of it. Let's move on.

We don't want your PC laptops—Sandy victims have gone through enough as it is. We don't want your khaki jacket with a corduroy collar. One word: Ew. We don't want your coat with the broken zipper. We don't want your pillow with drool rings. If I haven't been clear enough, go ahead and call me Mrs. Waterford because: Alena and Phil of North Babylon, NY. WE DON'T WANT YOUR CRAP!

Regards,

The Relief Volunteer You Made Dry Heave

Internal Monologue of the Overly Grateful Gas Station Attendant That I Tipped Only One Dollar

Dialogue:
"Oh, wow. Thank you. I really appreciate it. Thank you so much. I appreciate this one dollar. Thank you, thank you. I appreciate it."

Internal Monologue:
Wow. A dollar. I can't believe it. Thanks. I was just wondering how I would feed my wife and four children tonight, and now you've solved that little pickle. We can split a 5-piece Wendy's chicken nugget. Fantastic. That's almost one nugget each.

A dollar. It's like a dream come true. I don't know what to do first. Break it into four quarters? Save it and double down on a vending machine Powerade? Oh, the possibilities.

Is that a new pea coat you're wearing?

A dollar. Incredible. Muchas freaking gracias.

Nice car. It smells paid-off. I don't have a car myself. Kind of ironic for a guy who spends thirteen hours a day standing outside in the bitter cold of an early winter pumping people's gas for minimum wage while they sit comfortably in their heated paid-off Honda CRVs, huh? Yeah, life is full of fun little ironies just like that one.

This dollar is pretty crumpled. Like it was

smashed into the back pocket of a pair of expensive jeans—like it didn't even mean that much to you. But that can't be true because, by golly, it's a dollar! You just spent $30 of them having me fill up your car. You must be going somewhere very important to spend that kind of money. Is someone bleeding in your backseat? Do you have a meeting with the President? I assume you aren't doing something superfluous, like coming from a relaxing evening at an overpriced Italian restaurant, because that would be wasteful, and dollars—even single dollars—are an extremely valuable commodity.

Thank you again for this wrinkled dollar. I appreciate it. You have no idea. It will go such a long way. With only two thousand one hundred and ninety nine more, I might make rent this month. Or I can buy stale bread off the clearance shelf. Or I can ride a New York City subway in the 1980's.

I have no limits.

Oh, wait. I do. Anything over a dollar.

Thanks a lot, cheapskate. Enjoy your expertly pumped gas.

Benedict, By Vatican

"An Italian perfume maker was commissioned to create The Pope's cologne. The exact formula is top secret but it's rumored to have hints of lime, verbena and grass— reflecting the pontiff's love of nature."
– NPR

To the Newly Appointed Suffragan of Scents,

Our Gregorian chant-a-gramers reported that they reached you at home last night to commission you to this venerable position. So, now you know. The Vicar of Christ, the Supreme Pontiff, the Successor of St. Peter— The Pope—thinks he smells. And, as his Prime Minsniffer, I must agree. His Holiness is getting a bit.... stale. Like a Barberini Gospel, am I right? Anyway, we've collectively determined that his God-given odor falls short of capturing the outdoorsy essence of his character (no offense to The Big Guy), and this must be remedied.

Just so we are clear, the Governor of the World has a very specific vision for his signature fragrance. You are just the alchemist, not the artist. If you were thinking something tropical like coconut or pineapple, just forget it. You wouldn't find the Master Pastor lying poolside listening to Jimmy Buffet, so why would he smell like a piña colada? We want an aroma reminiscent of foliage. An olfactic medley of leaves and flowers, with a subtle note of citrus. An eau de Tree of Life, without the stink of sin.

As for the bottling design, the papal command is a golden mitre, the taller the better. We are looking for ornate, but a natural ornate. Think Renaissance man meets pastoral poet. And no head, just the really tall hat.

Now for the name. We aren't interested in anything cutesy like Holy Toilet Water, Very Vatican, or Pope-pourri. We're thinking something elegant, like Papa. No, scratch that. Benedict. Simple, classy, sophisticated. It's righteous.

Well, there's nothing left to say but welcome to the Cologne Council. Oh, and if you mess this up, there will be Hell to pay.

Sincerely His,
Servant of the servant of God's Prime Minsniffer

Quit Playing Games With My Heart, *The New Yorker*

Oh, *The New Yorker.*

Wasn't it you who pursued me two years ago, showing up on my doorstep, without any provocation, to court me, using the utmost seduction: offering me a "professional's rate," calling me a writer at a time when no one else did? I didn't ask you to come. I don't even like politics and, to be honest, I only skim over your many articles about countries and their governments. But you approached me and won me over with your cartoons, book/movie reviews, and, like I mentioned, by using flowery and confusing language like "professional."

Was it all lies? Is that what you tell every potential subscriber, just to get in their wallets? I really thought you saw something in me, that I was special. But now I wonder if I'm nothing more than a notch on your readership, an address on your mailing list.

Because, if you really thought I was a professional writer, you'd accept my proposals. You wouldn't be so afraid of committing to my submissions. I'd be Alena Dillon of *The New Yorker* by now. But no, I'm just Alena Dillon—has a professional's rate.

I really thought last week's would be the one. I imagined myself on a gorgeous white satiny page, standing before all of our family and friends, uniting with you, *The New Yorker*, for life. But then I got your email: This isn't right for us despite its evident merit.

At first I didn't believe the whole, "It's not you, it's me" bit. I read and reread my submission, thinking, *What's wrong with it, with me? Am I being too pushy? Is the prose not pretty enough?*

But then my Yahoo homepage lit up with an article from the *The New York Observer* titled, "Is *The New Yorker* a Total Bro-Fest?" which discussed the skewed proportion of male to female writers appearing in the publication. And, suddenly, it all made perfect sense. *The New Yorker,* you're into dudes. Not that there's anything wrong with that, I just wish you had been upfront with me from the start.

I want you to know that there are no hard feelings (at least not on my end). After all, I always wanted a magazine to bring with me to the spa.

Sincerely,
Alena Dillon—has a professional's rate

Breaking the Scale

Alena being debriefed on the Scale Mission

It took a year of steady interrogation, but the scale finally gave up the information I've been looking for. At first it laughed in my face, glowing a steady, red 146.5. That's the number it stuck with for months, confident and sure. Some claimed I needed to change my tactics. Incorporate exercise and healthy eating habits into my questioning. But I knew this was futile, a waste of time and ice cream. The scale would eventually break and give me what I wanted. So I persevered.

I applied heavy pressure over the course of the next six to eight months, stepping on its face at least once a day, sometimes twice. Sometimes three times. Sometimes I'd press it for the information, ease up, and press again immediately after, hoping for a different answer. This yielded little success. Around the end of 2011, this constant abuse only pissed the scale off, and it antagonized me by blinking 200, and occasionally ERROR. Maybe I was grilling it too hard too often, and it couldn't take the pressure. Maybe its energy was depleted. But I was convinced that the scale was just putting up a front, playing dead to get out of further interrogation. I would not be distracted from my mission, although I'd often leave the closet (where we kept the scale cordoned off) and exert my frustration on an entire bag of Kettle Corn popcorn. I sat at the kitchen table and shot nasty looks down the hall toward the closet as I stuffed fist full after fist full of salty sweet snack food into my mouth. I'm fairly confident that the scale couldn't hear my whimpering, but maybe it's smarter than I gave it credit for because it seemed to display knowledge of these binges the next time we met.

I think the real turning point was when our comforter, which was also stored in the closet, ripped, and I called JCPenney to see if it was too late to return it. While on the phone with the store rep, I glanced at the scale and my eyes said, 'It's not too late to return you either, scale. Don't think I won't bring you back to that dirty sale bin at Kohl's. Is that what you want? Give up the information or else.'

I let it stew in fear for a while, and didn't confront it again until the next morning. Obviously emotionally unstable, it flickered erratically—163, 141, 180, 197. Then the bottom half blacked out. I stomped my foot to wake it back up, and it flashed 123. A beautiful number. A number I never expected was possible. A number I haven't seen in decades.

Satisfied, I stepped off the scale and, in one last cry for mercy, it flashed "BATT." I said, "Okay scale, now that you've finally decided to cooperate, I'll see what I can do about the fresh batteries but, once you're refueled, you better not give me more of that 146.5 bullshit, or we'll start this interrogation over from the beginning."

Some say that this information, this overnight drop in twenty-three pounds, means nothing since it was acquired through torture. The scale was distressed and would have given me anything I wanted just to make me stop. I choose to ignore those claims. All I know is that today I looked down and saw my dream weight. Did you?

On Defending Myself Against Fame

"A famous writer who wants to continue writing has to be constantly defending himself against fame."
- Gabriel Garcia Marquez

I'd like to dedicate this essay to Nobel-prize winning author Gabriel Garcia Marquez, writer of *Love in the Time of Cholera* and *One Hundred Years of Solitude*, two classic novels that millions of high school and college students around the world never read but wrote papers on.

Being that it is his birthday, after all, and he has a few accomplishments from which I can learn, I've decided to take some time to really consider his advice. After all, I am a writer with more than one publication that tens of people have seen and maybe even enjoyed, so perhaps it is important to construct a defense strategy against the onslaught of fame that is sure to be riding a tsunami-sized wave this way. I must brace myself.

Before I'm prepared to combat the beast of my celebrity, I'll need to assess the size of the thing, what kind of teeth it bares, the nature of its prowess. Thus begins my quest.

The first stop on my odyssey is the sacred realm of Amazon, a land that monitors and cradles knowledge dear to all writers: the success of books. I don't actually have any published books, so I know this stop will be quick, although worthwhile.

I do, however, have an essay in an anthology (which will remain nameless), so I journey to this book's listing to expose myself to what I am sure will be pages and pages of reviews confessing how my essay is a life-changing read. Here will be where I will discover my fans, and after gauging their magnitude, I can begin to buy the supplies for, and then build, my figurative fame fortress.

When I type in the exact title of the anthology and click *enter*, a funny thing happens. It isn't the first book in the results. Or the second. It is the third. No bother, I venture on.

Yes, just as I expected. Customer reviews. What? Only four? Well it certainly is not about the quantity of fans, but the quality, the enthusiasm they have for me in their hearts. These four reviews must be soliloquies in my honor, beautiful language singing my praises. I scan for my name. How strange, nothing. They want to keep me, the object of their adoration, anonymous. Well, I can appreciate that. It is probably for my benefit, so that my life isn't swamped with paparazzi and, to Marquez's point, so that I can continue gifting the world with my contributions. I scan for the name of my essay. Hmmm. I scan for any key words that relate to the subject of my essay. Yes! Bullying!! All four reviews mention bullying. They do love me after all!

But I am hit by a pang of doubt. Could other essays in this anthology have also been about bullying? The anthology was geared toward pre-teens, could bullying possibly be a common theme? Almost sure that, no, I am a revolutionary, I turn to my contributor copy, flip to the table of contents, and my stomach drops. There is an entire section with essays about bullying—and my essay isn't even in that section! I am sorted in a completely different category. These reviewers are not my fans after all.

It is here that my investigative expedition meets its untimely end, and with less than glamorous findings.

On the bright side, since I am not defending

myself against fame, I can write uninhibited—free to create, write, revise, and repeat with NO limitations holding me back! Well, except for maneuvering around the blockades reserved for not famous writers—like years dedicated to sending queries and submissions so as to try to get noticed... oh, and the little factor of needing another job to support ourselves. Well, at least we aren't famous! That would really be hindering, wouldn't it?

To All Anti-Left-Ites

Left-handedness is not a choice—it's a quality people are born with. You think they would choose to be left-handed? You think that's the easy way out? No, not in this right-handed society. Not in this world where every left-handed schoolchild is forced to sit unnaturally in a right-handed desk; where they must train themselves to use scissors meant for an inherently different kind of person; where they can never fairly arm-wrestle. Even the most fundamental interaction with our fellow man—a handshake—is a constant reminder that lefties are not, and never will be, the norm. It takes a special kind of bravery for a left-handed person to constantly introduce him or herself to their fellow man with a lie.

Society claims to be tolerant, saying, "Oh, I'm not leftist. I have friends who are left-handed." It's a nice sentiment, but if our culture really understood, we would stop looking at lefties with disgust as they write with their hands curled around a pencil (I know it looks gross, but have some compassion). What's worse are those ignorant individuals who argue that handedness isn't even an issue anymore, saying things like, "We have a left-handed President, how much more hand tolerant can we get?" Just the fact that someone could boast tolerance when we live in a world where all left-handed people are still marked with lead smudges on their pinkies proves that this topic requires greater awareness.

When was the last time you heard, "Now raise your left hand?" or "Place your left hand over your heart?" Never. Your left hand never vows or pledges. Our society systematically distrusts all things left-handed, as evidenced in the expression "a left-handed compliment," which, despite how we claim to be a politically correct nation, still remains an accepted idiom—as if the left-handed are inherently more deceptive than the right-handed. Try telling Julius Caesar (left-handed) that he has more guile than Marcus Junius Brutus (right-handed). Go ahead, try!

Still incredulous about this prejudice? Well, answer me this: Do we have rights? Yes. Do they have lefts? No! Can our wrongs be righted? Yes. Can their wrongs be lefted? No!

Really, still not seeing it? Well, would you rather be left behind or right behind? Have you ever been grooving on the dance floor only to be told that you have two right feet? No, I didn't think you have.

What lefties need is a spokesperson—a famous face for left-handedness. How about Tom Cruise? No, too controversial; we'd lose support from pro-height people. How about Jerry Seinfeld? Yes, yes, he's likable, and I can't think of any additional bigotry he'd incite. Together with Jerry, let's send out a call to arms to put our hands together.

Lefties should no longer use a can opener or a stick shift or a baseball glove with shame. That's right, I mean, left! They're here, they're...er...get used to it!

I am a proud left-handedness activist. To join the movement, raise your left fist in solidarity.

Le Tour Defraud

Bonjour, et bienvenue. For those hailing from outside the civilized world, learn French you unnecessarily hygienic ignoramuses.

Before we commence today's tour through the creations of one of France's most treasured sons—and unopposed holder of Wikipedia's "Bearded Beret" title—we wish to pretend to regret to inform you that half of the Rodin Museum is closed for renovation, but we are pleased to announce that you will still be visiting the partial museum at full price.

Although the great masterpieces are not available for viewing, please take comfort in learning they remain somewhere on the premises, so you can go home and tell your family and friends that, in a way, you were in the presence of genius.

We acknowledge you paid full admission price under the pretense that you would admire his famous works. This is not a surprise to us as we are strategically making this renovation statement after your nonrefundable transaction. It may help to remember art is priceless. Except, of course, for the mandatory fee at which we've valued it.

Allow me to offer some further advice—don't dwell on our faux pas. It would be a waste of your precious time. You are in Paris, for God's sake! Home of the Eiffel Tower, the crusty baguette, and the sophisticated pout. There are plenty of other attractions out there just waiting for their chance to dupe you.

To buoy your disappointment, we here at Chateau Rodin have made a Continental effort to fill the gaps created by missing gems with some extra crap we found on museum grounds.

On your right is the first objet d'art, for which we use the words objet and art rather loosely. It may appear to be only a scrap of plaster, but curators have been paid to believe that this is a scrap of plaster the artist might have touched. Word to the wise, and to the Canadians: There isn't much to see in this museum so, to get your money's worth, we recommend lingering as much as you can stand. Don't just glance at the junk. Like a fine Bordeaux, give its insignificance time to mature. Look closer. See the corner? Inside that crevice? Some say if the lighting is just right and you've had enough to drink, you can see the Virgin Mary's face there. On the other hand, some say you can't.

You may be familiar with Rodin's statue *The Age of Bronze*, a life size nude male cast in 1876. In lieu of displaying this particular piece, we have a doorknob. We chose this item to represent the statue because many doorknobs are also made of bronze. This one, however, is not. It is of glass. It sounded like a good idea five minutes ago, when I tossed it on that rattletrap of a TV table, but the stand-in seems silly now. I would be embarrassed except I am French and unfamiliar with that particular sentiment.

This is a tissue used by Rodin—not the artist, the museum security guard we nicknamed Rodin (or Rody for short), coined for The Thinker pose he assumes on the toilet without ever locking the bathroom stall. It may interest you to know that some of my more vulgar colleagues call this pose, The Stinker.

And now for the pièce de résistance: an exit sign. Rodin met the original sculptor (became cadaverous, went to his narrow bed, fell to room temperature, bought a pine condo) sometime in the early 1900's, before the rise of exit signs (although don't quote me on that; I don't claim to be an expert). Because Rodin was around before exit signs became so popular, it can be argued that the whole concept of exit signs can be attributed to the innovations of his lifetime. It would be an argument based on zero evidence, but that doesn't mean it couldn't be argued. Don't think on it too hard. It's art; just let it do what it's supposed to do. Inspire.

Acknowledgements

I'd first like to recognize my publisher and friend, Colin D. Halloran, for taking me in from the cold and giving me a house and home.

I'm grateful to my parents for so many reasons; one of which being, in a bad economy, they paid for an English degree of all things without complaint. That's unconditional love. And to my brothers, Greg and Ryan, who are hilarious themselves and who always make me feel funny even when my jokes fall flat. I'm so blessed to be part of our family.

Thank you to Jennifer Walsh for her invaluable insights on these essays and Bill Patrick for strengthening my literary funny bone. In fact, I'd like to recognize all friends who have ever read my manuscripts. (I could try to name these people here but am sure to forget somebody and agonize over that oversight for the rest of my days. So instead, if you've ever read one of my manuscripts, I'm talking to YOU.) I'm sure your support often required restraint and poise, and I appreciate it.

And to Phil, the man I married, who has seen me at my worst, curled up on the couch in a ball of anxiety and self-doubt, or running around the apartment in a frenzy of anxiety and self-doubt, and yet never doubted me himself—at least not out loud. (He's also a damn good editor for a math brain.) What can I say? It's a gift to know you're the rest of my life.

22473941R00148

Made in the USA
Charleston, SC
20 September 2013